A NEW PARADIGM FOR "TRUE MENTAL HEALTH":

A STUDY OF MODELS OF MENTAL HEALTH AND ILLNESS WITH AN APPRAISAL FROM THE UNIFICATION THOUGHT PERSPECTIVE; TOWARD A GOD-CENTERED PARADIGM

by

Paula Petersen-Fujiwara, MRE, DMin.

First Printing: 2013

ISBN 978-1490489780

Dr. Paula Petersen-Fujiwara

Paulafuji3@juno.com

ACKNOWLEDGMENTS

My journey toward the accomplishment of this dissertation establishing a Unification Thought model of mental health and illness began in June of 2008 when I had a transformative experience that liberated me from chronic depression. I realized that my depression was caused by a vicious cycle of self-accusation thinking which could be broken through recognizing wrong thinking habits and changing them, that is, through confessing and repenting. I then decided to participate in a 40 day Cheongpyeong training center workshop beginning in July of that year. There, Dr. David Carlson, who had been one of my professors at the Unification Theological Seminary twenty years earlier, planted the thought in my mind to pursue a doctoral degree at Cheongshim Graduate School of Theology which is located near the Cheongpyeong training center. During that training period, I also received a calling from God to express in writing His viewpoint about mental health and illness. (True Parents' thought is just beginning to be systematically applied to psychology or the mental health field.) Although I hold no degree in psychology, I have experienced mental illness to varying degrees over a 40 year period of my life and have tried in several ways to deal with it including medication and group therapy. I have come to put my belief and trust in the spiritual works of the Cheongpyeong Heaven and Earth Training Center and have realized gradual and steady improvement by restoring my ancestors and liberating resentful spirits attached to me during training and "ansu" sessions. I have found that my mind has become clearer, purer and more focused and I have been able to more readily identify and change negative habits of thinking and feeling.

I promised to fulfill God's calling although I did not know how I would "make it happen." Within a year's time, God opened a few doors allowing me to gain employment in Korea and be accepted into the Doctor of Ministry program at Cheongshim Graduate School of Theology in 2009 and 2010 respectively.

I cannot express adequate gratitude to God, True Parents, Heung Jin nim, Dae Mo nim, Hoon Mo nim, and the faculty of Cheongshim Graduate School of Theology for creating and pioneering Cheongpyeong Heaven and Earth Training Center and Cheongshim Graduate School of Theology. I am a most blessed and privileged person to be allowed to grow spiritually, research, and write in this "Heaven on Earth" environment.

Developing this dissertation has been a great challenge, partly because I am not an experienced academician. However, I have trusted that my lacking points would be "filled in" by my passion and the assistance of Heaven and my restored ancestors and husband in the spirit world.

I especially thank Pres. Jin Choon Kim for recommending that I create categories for the systematic comparison of various models of mental health and illness as a way to highlight the more comprehensive and God-centered Unification Thought perspective. Also, my advisor, Dr. David Carlson has been like an elder brother to me throughout my time in the Doctor of Ministry program.

It is my hope and expectation that this dissertation can act as a catalyst for like-minded individuals to collaborate in the development of the paradigm for "true mental health" proposed in these pages. I gratefully and humbly offer this dissertation as my unique contribution for the establishment and expansion of Cheon Il Guk, the Kingdom of Heaven on Earth.

CONTENTS

CHAPTER II   THE UNIFICATION THOUGHT MODEL: A HOLISTIC AND COMPREHENSIVE PERSPECTIVE

CHAPTER III   APPRAISAL OF THREE MODELS FROM THE UNIFICATION THOUGHT PERSPECTIVE

INTRODUCTION

There is a great need today for an appraisal of the various approaches taken for the promotion of mental health and the treatment of mental illness. This is because these various approaches are not well-harmonized due to their opposing metaphysical assumptions and the partial world views associated with them. As a result, mental illness---which has afflicted people throughout human history---has yet to be cured and is, in fact, spreading more rampantly as time passes. Moreover, some treatment approaches in use today are doing more harm than good due, in large part, to their erroneous and unproven theoretical assumptions.

Unification Thought, originating from the teachings of the Reverend Dr. Sun Myung Moon and systematized by his disciple, Dr. Sang Hun Lee, we wish to propose as a systematic framework with which to appraise the various models for the maintenance of mental health and the treatment of mental disorders. The Unification Thought perspective provides a comprehensive and holistic framework which is helpful for understanding mental health and illness and which is capable of integrating and harmonizing physical, spiritual, and energetic perspectives. This could conceivably lead to improved mental health maintenance, to more efficacious treatment of mental illness, and ultimately, to a cure for all mental disorders.

This study utilizes the following categories for a systematic comparison of four models of mental health and illness: Western, Eastern, the human energy fields (aura), and the proposed model based upon Unification Thought:

1. Explanation of the ideal human being
2. The relationship between the mind and body
3. The structure of the mind and human nature
4. The definition of mental health and mental illness
5. The influence of family and environment on mental health
6. Approach for mental health maintenance
7. Approach for treatment of mental illness
8. The goal of therapy
9. qualifications of the therapist/counselor/healer

We will first examine these models under the broad headings of Western (psychology and psychiatry), Eastern (Asian religions), and the alternative approach for healing the human energy fields (aura) which is guided by the holism perspective. Then, we will present the proposed Unification Thought (UT) model. The UT model is able to clarify how the commonly accepted definitions of mental health in the fields of psychology and psychiatry can be achieved and maintained and, at the same time, resonates with the Eastern and human energy field healing approaches.

Next, we will critically compare the aforementioned models with the UT perspective in order to point out their limitations and strengths. Through this process, it will become apparent that it is possible for the Unification Thought model to resolve the limitations of the other models as well as integrate and harmonize the strengths of these physical, spiritual, and energetic perspectives.

In conclusion, the basic tenets of the UT model will be summarized and presented as a new paradigm for attaining "true mental health." And finally, possible future directions for research and development of this new paradigm will be delineated.

CHAPTER I   THREE MODELS OF MENTAL HEALTH AND ILLNESS

1. THE WESTERN MODEL OF MENTAL HEALTH AND ILLNESS (psychology and psychiatry)

1) Explanation of an ideal human being

Since the founding of modern psychology, theorists have attempted to describe and analyze human behavior from many perspectives including materialism, mechanism, naturalism, determinism, hedonism and relativism. Since the mid-20th century, the disease model of human functioning has been prevalent, focusing on mental and behavioral dysfunction. More recently, positive psychology has come into vogue with an emphasis on human virtues and how one can attain happiness. However, there has been no emphasis concerning a theory of an ideal human being among Western theorists.[1]

2) Explanation of the Relationship between the Human Mind and Body

There are many schools of thought within the field of psychology regarding the relationship of the human mind and body and, more specifically, between the mind and the physical brain. This relationship has come to be known in philosophy as the "mind-brain problem." There are two basic theories (with many sub-variants) known as monistic materialism and dualism. "Monistic materialism thinks the world consists of material only. Mind is only an epiphenomenon of materialistic activities. On the other hand, dualism posits two different kinds of being: mind and matter. These interact through the brain. Most scientists take the monistic materialism position."[2]

In the late 19th century, the pioneers of modern psychology adopted the prevailing world view of scientific naturalism instead of the Christian world view which was centered upon the dualism of spirit and matter because they wanted to establish a respected field of science.

---

[1] P. Scott Richards and Allen Bergin, *A Spiritual Strategy for Counseling and Psychotherapy*, 2nd ed. (Washington, D.C.: American Psychological Association, 2005), 61.

[2] Hiroshi Ishii, *The Mind-Brain Problem and Unification Thought,* (Seoul: Unification Thought Institute, 2008), 11.

Proponents of "naturalism...assume that human beings and the universe can be understood and eventually fully explained without including God or divine influence in the scientific theories or in the interpretation of research findings."[3] It should be noted that western philosophy based on the Christian world view and scientific naturalism have differing philosophical assumptions about existing beings:

> The Western Christian philosophical tradition of spirit finds its roots in Plato's division of existing beings into form and matter. In this view matter is the continuous material 'stuff' of the being, and form is the intangible and non-material idea or pattern of the being. For Plato the forms exist independently of material beings in their own realm. In human beings he equates form with mind and soul, and this equality has stuck. Since then the concept of spirit has been wedded to that of immaterial mind and is the common Western and Christian perception of spirit. ...Spirit is thus undetectable, indivisible, and from the perspective of natural science, must be devoid of energy. This leads to a conception of the human being as a dualism of immaterial mind/spirit and material body. ...[T]he traditional conception of spirit as immaterial mind devoid of energy makes it completely undetectable by any conceivable means, so in principle science cannot even begin to address this issue. It cannot completely deny this concept of spirit, but equally cannot hope to prove it either.[4]

"Many people at this time believed that science, not religion, would unlock all the mysteries of the universe."[5] However, the scientific method only observes physical phenomena and has no point of reference for studying spiritual phenomena as long as it is believed that spirit has no substance or energy. Thus, the ontological gap between traditional western philosophy and modern psychology has led to the human spirit or consciousness being ignored or denied by many theorists in the field of psychology. This may explain why the predominant view of the relationship of mind and body in the fields of psychology and psychiatry is based on the theory of materialistic monism wherein mental activity is thought to arise solely from the physical brain.

---

[3] Richards and Bergin, *A Spiritual Strategy,* 37.

[4] David Burton, "What is the Spirit?: Some Physics of Spiritual Existence." *The Unity of Sciences and Unification Thought* Vol.8 (2006): 293-94.

[5] Richards and Bergin, *A Spiritual Strategy,* 37.

3) The Structure of the Mind and Human Nature

(1) The Structure of the Mind

There are many theories concerning the attributes of the human mind that are continually debated. Attributes which are commonly cited are those of reason, intelligence, thought, emotion, memory, and personality. In the western world, the most well-known theory defining the attributes of the human mind was developed by Sigmund Freud (1856-1939), the founder of modern psychology. He theorized that at the core of the mind there is libido or sexual energy that flows out from the id, which is like a reservoir for this energy. Then there is the ego which functions as the attribute of reason which has to repress the id.[6]

(2) View of Human Nature

The early pioneers of modern psychology were Sigmund Freud who developed psychoanalytical theory and J.B. Watson, the founder of behavioral psychology. They and many of their adherents were atheists who believed in scientific naturalism and the Newtonian "clockwork" understanding of the physical universe and so their theories were materialistic, mechanistic, reductionistic, and deterministic.[7] For example, in early behavioral theory "it was believed that human behavior could be explained and reduced to stimulus-response connections and that only observable behavior was considered real.[8] A human being was a materialistic 'machine' that was completely controlled by environmental influences."[9]

Darwin's theory of evolution also influenced Freud and the early behaviorists. "They rejected the notion that there are transcendent moral and ethical principles that can or should

---

[6] Akifumi Otani, "Beyond Freudianism," *The Unity of Sciences and Unification Thought: Towards Exploring Unification Thought Academic Disciplines*, (2011), 1.

[7] Ibid., 40.

[8] J.B. Watson, *Psychology from the Standpoint of a Behaviorist*, (Dover, NH: Frances Pinter, 1983 Original work published in 1924), quoted in Richards and Bergin, *A Spiritual Strategy*, 39.

[9] L. Krasner, "The Therapist as a Social Reinforcement Machine," *Research in Psychotherapy* vol. 2, eds. H.H. Strupp & L. Luborsky, (Washington, D.C.: American Psychological Association, 1962), quoted in Richards and Bergin, *A Spiritual Strategy*, 39.

optimize human behavior and social relations"[10] and instead characterized human nature as similar to the rest of the animal kingdom.

Opposition to this viewpoint came from a movement known as humanist-existential psychology led by Abraham Maslow and Carl Rogers. "This movement gave hope to those who viewed human behavior as being more complex and potentially agentive, as reflecting the potential for actualization espoused in the aspirations of idealistic religions. This movement opened the way for alternative conceptions of human functioning."[11] There were also psychologists and psychiatrists who wrote more explicitly about religion including William James, Carl Jung, Victor Frankl, and M. Scott Peck. This stimulated a continuously developing pastoral counseling movement.[12]

By the mid-1970's, mainstream psychology had ...revised its earlier views concerning consciousness and the subjective, replacing long dominant behaviorist theory with a new mentalist or cognitive paradigm. This changeover...has now legitimized the contents of inner experience, such as sensations,...thoughts, feelings, and the like, as...causal constructs in the scientific explanation of brain function and behavior.[13] The development of alternative psychotherapy traditions..., the movement toward psychotherapy integration,...the recognition of the importance of values in psychotherapy, and the development of spiritually oriented treatment approaches have challenged naturalistic, deterministic, relativistic, and hedonistic views of human nature and methods of therapeutic change.[14]

4) Definition of Mental Health and Mental Illness

(1) Definition of Mental Health

The commonly accepted definitions of mental health in modern psychology include the following:

---

[10] Richards and Bergin, *A Spiritual Strategy*, 39.

[11] Ibid., 40.

[12] Ibid.

[13] R.W. Sperry, "Psychology's Mentalist Paradigm and the Religion/Science Tension," *American Psychologist*, 43 (1988): 607-613, quoted in Richards and Bergin, *A Spiritual Strategy*, 58.

[14] Richards and Bergin, *A Spiritual Strategy*, 49-50.

1. absence of mental illness, that is, a stable mind with an ability to function adequately

2. appropriate social behavior, that is, behavior that is not disruptive in social settings

3. freedom from worry and guilt, that is, not incapacitated by extreme anxiety, but rather relatively carefree

4. personal competence and control, that is, self-disciplined

5. self-acceptance and self-actualization, that is, self-confident and able to develop one's innate potential talents and abilities

6. unification and organization of personality, that is, a relative balance of intellect, emotion, and will

7. open-mindedness and flexibility, that is, relatively unbiased and without rigid thinking[15]

(2) Definition of Mental Illness

Since the fields of psychology and psychiatry depend solely on the scientific method which has no basis for understanding or addressing the human spirit or consciousness, their diagnoses and prescriptions for treatment are dependent more on theories and descriptions of symptoms than on known causes of mental disorders. This fact is readily admitted in the introduction of the *Diagnostic and Statistical Manual of Mental Disorders (DSM),* a manual developed by the American Psychiatric Association since the early 1960s as a guide for psychiatrists in diagnosing mental disorders. To the point:

> For most of the DSM-III disorders…the etiology is unknown. A variety of theories have been advanced, buttressed by evidence---not always convincing—to explain how these disorders come about.[16]

It is also stated in the introduction that "[a]lthough this manual provides a classification of mental disorders, there is no satisfactory definition that specifies precise boundaries for the

---

[15] R.F. Paloutzian, *Invitation to the Psychology of Religion.* 2nd ed. (London: Allyn and Bacon, 1996), 253, quoted in John Swinton, *Spirituality and Mental Health Care: Rediscovering a 'Forgotten' Dimension.* (London: Jessica Kingsley Publishers, 2001), 35.

[16] Robert L. Spitzer, MD., *Diagnostic and Statistical Manual of Mental Disorders,* 3rd ed. (Washington, D.C., American Psychiatric Association, 1980), 6-7.

concept 'mental disorder.'"[17]

The dominant Western theory about the cause of mental illness is known as the medical or biological model of mental illness. This model posits that mental illness is a result of a chemical or neurotransmitter imbalance in the brain (such as dopamine or serotonin). In the West, pharmaceutical medications have been developed to improve and maintain the balance of a patient's brain chemicals.[18] There is some criticism of this hypothesis since no standard medical test is given to determine if a chemical imbalance is evident. Prescriptions for medications are usually given based on patient interviews and observation of symptomatic behavior rather than medical tests.[19]

5) The influence of Family and Environment on Mental Health

The influence on mental health of family relationships and the environment (both social and natural) have been studied using social scientific research methodology. It is generally recognized that strong families and pure environment promote mental health and that dysfunctional families and negative environmental influences induce mental illness.

6) The Approach for Mental Health Maintenance

As a result of financial incentives in the U.S.A. after World War II,

> ...psychologists became preoccupied with mental illness and adopted the disease model of human functioning. Accordingly, for the remainder of the 20th century, mainstream psychologists largely neglected the study of human strengths and virtues, leaving mental health professionals ill-equipped to facilitate normal human development or engage in effective prevention.[20]

---

[17] Ibid., 5.

[18] http://en.wikipedia.org/wiki/chemical_imbalance (accessed July 10, 2012)

[19] Gwen Olsen, "The Mission-Gwen Olsen -the Rx Reformer", http://www.youtube.com/watch?v=j4byng7x7Kk, (accessed July 10, 2012.)

[20] M.E.P. Seligman, "Positive Psychology, Positive Prevention, and Positive Therapy," *Handbook of Positive Psychology*, eds. C.R. Snyder & S.J. Lopez, (New York: Oxford University Press, 2002), 3-9, quoted in Richards and Bergin, *Spiritual Strategy*, 60.

> After becoming president of the American Psychological Association in 1997, M.E.P. Seligman shifted his focus from studying mental illness to understanding human strengths and virtues. He coined the term "positive psychology" and called on psychologists to change their focus 'from a preoccupation only with repairing the worst things in life to also building the best qualities in life.'[21]

Since then, there has been a growing interest in positive psychology in the mainstream mental health professions. These days, the majority of therapists are integrating various approaches including more holistic and spiritual therapies; tailoring them to the needs and the unique spirituality of their clients.[22]

7) The Treatment Approach for Mental Illness

Depending on the severity of the disorder, what is available with the Western model is individual, family or group therapy and counseling, pharmaceutical medication, or hospitalization with medication. It is the role of psychiatrists to diagnose disorders and prescribe medication. Psychotherapists provide psychotherapy to clients. Clinical psychologists mainly do research and mental health counselors provide counseling in various settings including mental health clinics, schools and large companies.[23]

8) The Goal of Therapy/Counseling

The goal of therapy or counseling varies depending on the therapy or counseling approach and its underlying assumptions about human nature and value system. As was pointed out in the discussion of the Western model's view of human nature, there has been a continuum of views ranging from materialistic to more spiritual which dictate what the desired outcome should be. For example, one therapist might guide his client to deny or overcome her guilt because it is not warranted from the standpoint of the therapist's secular value system while another more spiritually-inclined therapist might guide her client to confess and repent in order

---

[21] Ibid., 3.

[22] Richards and Bergin, *A Spiritual Strategy*, 61, 63.

[23] http://www.onetonline.org/link/summary/19-3031.03, accessed September 12, 2012.

to resolve guilty feelings.

9) Qualifications or Attributes of the Therapist/Counselor/Healer

There are many sub-specialties within the fields of psychology and psychiatry. Within the field of psychology, graduate-level studies are required with an emphasis in either research or applied (therapeutic) psychology. Psychiatrists have graduate-level medical training and must earn medical licenses. Licensing requirements vary on national and state or provincial levels.[24]

10) Summary of the Western model of mental health and illness:

(1) Explanation of an ideal human being

There has been no clear explanation or consensus among Western theorists concerning what an ideal human being would be like.

(2) The Relationship between the Mind and Body

The predominant view of the relationship between the mind and body is that mental activity arises from the physical brain. (monistic materialism)

(3) The Structure of the Human Mind and Human Nature

The Western field of psychology has many theories regarding the attributes of the mind. Thus far, no clear definition has been agreed upon concerning the structure of the mind. Since the pioneering of modern psychology, the view of human nature has shown a general trend from a materialistic paradigm toward a more spiritual paradigm. However, the view of human nature has yet to be clarified and has not found consensus in the field of psychology.

(4) Definition of Mental Health and Mental Illness

1. absence of mental illness, 2. appropriate social behavior, 3. freedom from worry and guilt, 4. personal competence and control, 5. self-acceptance and self-actualization, 6. unification and organization of personality, 7. open-mindedness and flexibility

---

[24] http://en.wikipedia.org/wiki/Mental_health_professional (accessed July 10, 2012)

The predominant paradigm for the cause of mental illness is the biological model which asserts that illness is the result of imbalanced brain chemicals.

(5) The influence of family and environment on mental health

It is generally recognized that strong families and pure environment promote mental health and that dysfunctional families and negative environmental influences induce mental illness.

(6) The approach for mental health maintenance

During the late 20th century there was a preoccupation with mental illness and the disease model for human functioning was prevalent, leaving mental health professionals ill-equipped to facilitate normal human development.

(7) The treatment approach for mental illness

The Western treatment approach emphasizes the prescription of pharmaceutical drugs in order to manage, but not cure, the imbalance of brain chemicals. There are many theories for psychotherapy which are integrated and tailored by therapists to the needs of each unique patient.

(8) The goal of therapy/counseling

The goal of therapy or counseling varies depending on the therapy or counseling approach and its underlying assumptions about human nature and value system.

(9) Qualifications of the therapist/counselor

Psychiatrists, who prescribe medication for mental disorders must hold graduate-level medical degrees. Psychologists, who do research or counsel patients, must hold graduate degrees in at least one of the social science majors.

Because the structure of the mind, the relationship of the mind and body, the view of human nature, and the cause and treatment of mental illness have yet to be clearly understood in the Western model of mental health and illness, this model is insufficient for curing mental illness and for achieving and maintaining mental health.

2. THE EASTERN MODEL OF MENTAL HEALTH AND ILLNESS (Asian Religions)

1) Explanation of the ideal human being

In Buddhism, an ideal person is an enlightened one possessing the Buddha nature which manifests as ethical conduct, mental discipline, wisdom, and compassion. From the Taoist perspective, an ideal person lives with simplicity, spontaneity, and naturalness according to the way of the universe. Confucius taught that human beings have natural goodness endowed by Heaven and an ideal person has a pure soul and a brilliant spirit.[25]

2) The Relationship between the Mind and Body

Unlike traditional Western philosophy, Asian philosophy does not recognize a dualism of a spirit or mind and a physical body which have nothing in common. On the contrary, Asian philosophy regards spirit, mind and body as an undivided continuum of energy. In fact, the entire cosmos is regarded as a continuum or web of vibrating energy emerging from and nurtured by what is referred to as "vital essence" or "pure consciousness."[26] All matter is thought to have some level of consciousness. Consciousness is considered as a more subtle form of matter. Thus, mind and body share common elements. Then, Asian philosophy disagrees with the dominant view in psychology that mental activity (consciousness) is somehow produced by the physical brain. The understanding of Asian philosophy is that every existing being including the human brain arises from cosmic consciousness and is imbued with consciousness.[27]

3) The structure of the mind and human nature

In Asian culture and religion there is no clear determination of specific attributes of the

---

[25] David Carlson, Paths of Faith in Providential Perspective, lecture presentation on April 26, 2010.

[26] Sir John Woodroffe, *The Serpent Power* (New York: Dover, 1974), 33, quoted in Michael Talbot, *The Holographic Universe* (New York: Harper Collins, 1991), 288; and Douglas Sharon, *Wizard of the Four Winds: A Shaman's Story*, (New York: Free Press, 1978), 59, quoted in Talbot, *The Holographic Universe*, 289.

[27] Ibid.

mind other than the recognition of the existence of the human ego. Buddhists speak of the delusion of the ego which brings about human suffering; the Confucian and Shinto traditions guide people to avoid being egoistic because we live in a social environment in which we are expected to fulfill our roles and responsibilities.

In Asian philosophy there is an ancient concept that the cosmos is composed of two fundamental forces known as the yang and yin which interact in a complementary relationship to create a dynamic (as opposed to static) balance. In the human consciousness yang characteristics are those of a masculine nature including activity, rational thinking, competition, aggressiveness, etc. The yin characteristics of a feminine nature include modes of consciousness which can be described as intuitive, religious, mystical, or psychic. Thus, within the human mind two basic types of thought are recognized: rational and intuitive.[28] "In many Eastern traditions the dynamic balance between the male and female modes of consciousness is the principal aim of meditation...."[29]

The forces of yang and yin form complementary pairs on every level of existence. As mentioned above, the yang and yin aspects of the mind, that is, the rational and intuitive aspects, follow the Tao or the cosmic way of harmonious and balanced interaction.[30]

According to Buddhist teaching, humans have an ordinary nature but by striving to overcome cravings and desires, as well as the delusions of the ego and ignorance through the Eightfold Path it is possible to attain the Buddha nature.[31] The ordinary nature fundamentally manifests as greed, hatred and delusion.[32] The attributes of the Buddha Nature are ethical conduct, mental discipline, wisdom, and compassion.[33] One who has reached enlightenment is thus able to perceive, experience and interact with the world without the ceaseless cravings and ego attachments of the ordinary nature.[34]

In Taoism, undesirable things such as greed, disease, and war are caused by not knowing

---

[28] Fritjof Capra, *The Tao of Physics: An Exploration of the Parallels Between Modern Physics and Eastern Mysticism* (New York: Bantam Books, 1975), 133.

[29] Ibid.

[30] Ibid.

[31] David Carlson, Paths of Faith, lecture presentation on April 5, 2010.

[32] Mark Epstein, *Thoughts without a Thinker: Psychotherapy from a Buddhist Perspective* (New York: Basic Books, 1995),19.

[33] Gary Groth-Marnat, "Buddhism and Mental Health: A Comparative Analysis," in *Religion and Mental Health,* ed. John F. Schumaker (New York: Oxford University Press, 1992), 272.

[34] Ibid.

or following or actively opposing the Tao which is the way of the universe. One should return to the uncorrupted way of nature by living with simplicity, spontaneity, and naturalness.[35]

Confucius believed that humans have natural goodness endowed by Heaven but that it needs to be nurtured in order to be realized and fulfilled. He taught that impropriety in relationships is the core human problem which can be remedied by developing a perfect social order through moral education. The fundamental concern in Confucianism is "learning to be human" through building character and thus actualizing a pure soul and a brilliant spirit.[36]

4) Definition of Mental Health and Mental Illness

In Asian philosophy, mental health is generally understood as the balanced and harmonized relationship of the rational and intuitive aspects of the mind. From the perspective of Shamanism, mental health is understood as the absence of spiritual disturbance through maintaining harmony with the spirit world.

From the Buddhist perspective, the source of mental disturbance is ignorance of one's true self and the deceptions of the ego. According to the Buddha's Four Noble Truths, human suffering is experienced by all people and we are the cause of our own suffering. It is possible for us to become enlightened through the Noble Eightfold Path and, by that way, end our suffering.[37] However, the Buddha did not elucidate how humans came to be in this state of ignorance and ego delusion.

Taoism recognizes that undesirable things happen if one is not in alignment with the Tao, the natural and spontaneous way of the universe. Confucius regarded impropriety to be the fundamental cause of disorder within individuals and society. However, although he taught that humans are inherently good, he did not explain why humans tend to behave improperly.

Shamanism is an ancient religion that is still practiced in many Asian cultures. The shaman is a spiritualist, a specialist in the human soul who can control spirits in the spirit realm and serves to protect his or her community from spiritual disturbances since it is believed that there are spirits everywhere constantly affecting human beings both mentally and physically. People's problems are understood to have their origin in the spirit realm and it is the shaman's

---

[35] Carlson, Paths of Faith, lecture presentation on April 26, 2010.
[36] Ibid., May 3, 2010.
[37] Groth-Marnat, "Buddhism and Mental Health", 271.

role to provide solutions through rituals and offerings to the spirits.[38] The traditions of shamanism are still practiced today throughout Asia so there is a prevailing belief that the cause of mental disorders originates from the spirit realm even though the Western model of mental illness---which generally ignores spiritual influences---has been imported to modern Asian societies.

5) The influence of family and environment on mental health

Buddhism's prescription for mental health centers exclusively on the individual's efforts to control his mind and the practice of non-attachment to desires of the ego. Therefore, many Buddhists choose to be celibate and live an ascetic single life close to nature. Confucianism focuses on "learning to be human" through education about proper family and societal relationships. Taoism focuses on learning the correct way to live through observing the ways of the natural world. Each approach promotes mental stability. Not following their teachings necessarily leads to suffering because human beings are ignorant of and not aligned with the way of Heaven.

6) The approach for mental health maintenance

The Buddhist way to achieve and maintain mental health is to follow the Eightfold Path:

> ...Right Understanding, Right Thought, Right Speech, Right Action, Right Livelihood, Right Effort, Right Mindfulness, and Right Concentration (meditation). Much of Buddhist teaching is an elaboration of how these guidelines can be incorporated into daily life.[39]

To be mentally healthy is to be aware but emotionally detached from the cravings and delusions of the ego and therefore to be free from them. This awareness is developed through meditation

---

[38] Carlson, Paths of Faith, lecture presentation on March 9, 2010.

[39] Groth-Marnat, "Buddhism and Mental Health," 272.

practice. One is also encouraged to "be in the moment" instead of ceaselessly dwelling in the past or worrying about the future. Many people in Buddhist cultures choose to live an ascetic life, even as a monk or nun in order to focus on attaining their true selves and to guide others to do the same.

Taoism and Confucianism do not directly address the nature of the human mind. Their focus is on aligning with the way of nature or moral and ethical norms. Shamans help people keep harmony with their ancestors and other spirits so that they can maintain their mental stability as well as their physical health.

7) The treatment approach for mental illness

From the Buddhist perspective:

> If an individual experiences pain and suffering, a spiritual answer is typically given. In a general way, this would involve understanding the person's craving and attachment in combination with explaining how their past actions (karma) had led them into the present state of their lives. In Buddhist beliefs, the mind, and indeed a person's sense of ego identity, are perceived as an illusion on ignorance. It is this ignorance that ultimately leads to suffering and a sense of separateness and alienation between people. A Buddhist would even perceive our "normal" sense of identity as being so distorted that we are unaware that it is a distortion. Thus, normality might even be conceptualized as a culture-wide neurosis, a "consensus trance," a collective psychosis.... The Buddhist cure for this state is by training the mind to go beyond the distortions and limits of normality and into a deeper sense of Truth. While Western psychology is concerned with relative mental health, Buddhism is more concerned with ultimate mental health.[40] ...[W]hen the nature of suffering is understood, it can be ended through nonattachment. While the formula is simple, achieving it requires an extremely high level of commitment, discipline, and practice.[41]

> Meditation has sometimes been referred to as the royal road to mental health. It is both a tool for exploring consciousness and a means of transforming it. Practitioners state that it is able to purge the mind of

---

[40] Groth-Marnat, "Buddhism and Mental Health", 270-71.

[41] Ibid., 271.

"mental toxins" (hostility, envy, greed, anger, etc.), create psychological harmony, and, as a result, enhance physical health. In addition, meditation is believed to increase personal control and self-restraint, while also facilitating right knowledge. ... The two basic strategies are to focus one's concentration (usually on a chant or on breathing), or to observe one's reactions in a mindful manner. Watching one's reactions during meditation requires that the practitioner note mental contents but suspend judgment over them. The contents are neither accepted nor rejected, and they are not placed into any categories of good or evil. ... The mental contents, many of which are emotionally charged, gradually become desensitized as the practitioner stops identifying with them.[42]

In Shamanism, to alleviate any kind of disease a ceremony with many rituals is performed in which prayers are said for the realization of the client's wishes. However, this method can only give comfort or reduce the problem temporarily, not permanently. Such ceremonies do not solve the problem fundamentally.[43]

8) Goal of Therapy/Counseling

The goal in following the Eightfold Path of Buddhism is to reach enlightenment and thus be liberated from cravings and delusions of the ego. It is to detach from desires which leads to "the spontaneous development of unconditional love (karuna), wisdom (prajna), and compassion. These qualities emerge when the person 'lets go.' They are not goals, but by-products."[44] "[T]ransforming suffering by changing the way we relate to it" is another way of expressing it.[45]

In Taoism, the goal of its discipline/practice is to align with the way of nature. In Confucianism the goal of its practice is to find the way of ancient virtue in order to create an orderly society of proper relationships. In Shamanism the goal of its practice is to bring humans from disharmony into harmony with the ancestors and the spirits.[46]

---

[42] G. Dubs, "Psycho-spiritual development in Zen Buddhism: A study of resistance in meditation" *Journal of Transpersonal Psychology,* 19 (1987), 19-87, quoted in Groth-Marnat, "Buddhism and Mental Health", 274-75.

[43] Carlson, Paths of Faith, lecture presentation on March 9, 2010.

[44] Groth-Marnat, "Buddhism and Mental Health", 273.

[45] Mark Epstein, *Thoughts without a Thinker,* 40.

[46] Carlson, Paths of Faith, lecture presentations in spring, 2010.

9) Qualifications or Attributes of the Therapist/Counselor/Healer

Adherents of Buddhism can receive guidance from celibate monks and ascetics by listening to Dharma talks or by experiencing "temple stays" for brief periods of time in order to receive meditation training. One unique aspect of Buddhism is the following:

> Buddhism, probably more than any other belief system, emphasizes that people are responsible for their own condition. This is true because of the principle of cause and effect) and because of belief in the potential for mental control.... If a person is in a certain situation, then it must be the result of some past action. By fully understanding these past actions, people can better perceive why they are involved in their current condition. ... Although the teacher (including Buddha himself) is initially helpful, even he will eventually be a hindrance. An ancient Buddhist saying is "Look within, you are the Buddha." Thus, no one can save another person other than oneself.[47]

However, there is also the Buddhist concept of the Bodhisattva of Compassion, an enlightened one who postpones his entrance to Nirvana in order to help humanity overcome suffering. Then, there is the Maitreya Buddha who is the Buddha who is expected to return to humanity. Also, Confucianism has an expectation that a True Man will come.[48]

The shaman is the counselor-healer of the Shamanist tradition. He or she becomes a shaman through inheritance, training, or calling. A shaman must do an apprenticeship with a mentor and learn all the many rituals and then undergo an initiation ritual. The more powerful shamans have extraordinary energy, mental acuity, and sensitivity.[49]

Those who would counsel, guide, or teach others in the Taoist and Confucianist traditions are those who are exemplary in the practice of their teachings.[50]

A fundamental purpose of any of the world's religions is to guide human beings to dominate their body's desires in order to free their minds and, more specifically, to empower

---

[47] Groth-Marnat, "Buddhism and Mental Health", 276-7.
[48] Carlson, Paths of Faith, lecture presentation on April 5, 2010.
[49] Carlson, Paths of Faith, lecture presentation on March 9, 2010.
[50] Carlson, Paths of Faith, lecture presentation on May 3, 2010.

their conscience, which is their innate moral guidance system endowed by their Creator.[51]

10) Summary of the Eastern model of mental health and illness:

(1) Explanation of the ideal human being

In Buddhism, an ideal person is an enlightened one. For Taoists, an ideal person lives according to the way of the universe. Confucius taught that human beings have natural goodness endowed by Heaven.

(2) The relationship between the mind and body

Our physical body, including the human brain, is seen as arising from cosmic consciousness. Mind and body are understood as parts of an undivided continuum of energy imbued with consciousness.

(3) The structure of the mind and human nature

Eastern thought understands the ideal structure of the human mind as the harmonious oneness of the dual attributes of yin and yang which are evident throughout the cosmos. This duality is expressed in the human mind as the rational and intuitive thought processes. In Buddhism, true human nature is the Buddha nature of ethical conduct, mental discipline, wisdom and compassion. From the Confucian perspective, human beings are naturally endowed with a good nature, but there is a tendency toward impropriety which needs to be overcome through moral education. Taoism teaches that humans are meant to align with the Tao or way of the universe.

(4) Definition of mental health and mental illness

Mental health is the balanced and harmonized relationship of the rational and intuitive aspects of the mind as well as the absence of spiritual disturbance. In Buddhism, we are the cause of our own suffering due to ignorance, cravings, and the deceptions of our ego. Confucius would say that impropriety is the root of disorder in human relationships. Taoism points to the lack of alignment with the Tao or way of nature as the root of human imbalance. Shamanism sees the influence of troublesome spirits in the spiritual realm as the source of mental disturbance.

---

[51] Carlson, Paths of Faith, lecture presentation on March 9, 2010.

(5) The influence of family and environment on mental health

To maintain mental stability, the focus of Buddhism is the individual, Confucianism focuses on family and societal relationships, and Taoism focuses on the natural world. Shamanism's focus is on harmony with the spirit world.

(6) The approach for mental health maintenance

The Buddhist Eightfold Path, particularly, mindful meditation practice, is the means for maintaining mental health. Shamans help people to stay in harmony with their ancestors and other spirits in order to maintain mental stability.

(7) The treatment approach for mental illness

In Buddhism, meditation is a tool for purging the mind of mental toxins such as greed, anger, and envy through nonattachment. Shamans conduct rituals and ceremonies to appease troublesome spirits.

(8) The goal of therapy

The goal of the Buddhist Eightfold Path is to achieve enlightenment. In Taoism, the goal is to align with the way of nature. In Confucianism the goal is to create an orderly society of proper relationships. In Shamanism the goal is to bring humans into harmony with the ancestors and the spirits.

(9) Attributes of the therapist/counselor/healer

Those who provide teaching, training, or treatment are highly spiritually evolved ascetics, sages or shamans.

Since Eastern philosophy does not elucidate the origin of cravings, ignorance, impropriety, or evil spiritual influence which it identifies as the roots of humanity's mental suffering, it cannot provide a complete solution or "cure" for mental illness.

3. THE HOLISM/HUMAN ENERGY FIELD MODEL OF MENTAL HEALTH AND ILLNESS

1) Explanation of the ideal human being

An ideal human being is a manifestation of God. Such a person has a divine spark within him or herself and a connection with "divine mind." An ideal person is characterized as having harmonized rational and intuitive minds, self-acceptance, a capacity for expressing unconditional love in relationships, and a commitment to practicing the truth.[52]

2) The relationship between the mind and body

Beyond the physical plane there is the dimension of the universal or life energy field in the context of which the human energy fields exist and function. In India it is known as prana and the Chinese call it chi. This universal field "is the energetic framework or grid structure upon which the physical world rests."[53] Energy healers can perceive the human energy fields with what they call HSP or higher sense perception. Energy healers say that everything that exists in the physical dimension originates from these energy fields. Scientists often refer to human energy fields as bioenergy fields. Many scientists assume that these fields originate from the physical body but energy healers believe that these fields exist prior to the body and that the body is created by these fields. These fields hold the physical body together, provide it with life energy, and "serve as a communication and integration system that keeps the body functioning as a single organism."[54]

The attributes of the mind are seen to reside in the human energy fields. The human energy fields act as molds or templates for the physical body. Thus, it can be said that the mind has a cause and effect relationship with the physical body.

The understanding of the nature and function of the human energy fields comes from the holism perspective. The first premise of holism is that consciousness is the basic reality. The basic reality of the human energy fields is energy but, on a deeper level, there is intention or

---

[52] Barbara Brennan, *Light Emerging: The Journey of Personal Healing* (New York: Bantam Books, 1993), passim 19-26.
[53] Barbara Brennan, *Light Emerging*, 13.
[54] Ibid., 20.

purpose upon which our energy flow is based.[55] Energy healers recognize that the intention or purpose that guides the flow of energy in the universe originates from the source of our consciousness and potential for divinity, namely, God. Energy healer, Barbara Brennan states that:

> God is everywhere, in everything. ...The divine spark of God is uniquely individual in each of us. It is God individually manifested. We experience it as our inner fountain head, or the core of our being. ... When we are connected to the universal God and the individual God within, we are completely safe and free.[56]

3) The structure of the mind and human nature

As mentioned previously, the attributes of the human mind are not to be found confined within the physical brain, but are instead contained in the 7 fields or bodies of energy which, when properly cleared, charged and balanced, form a sphere that surrounds and penetrates the physical body. These energy fields/bodies have successively higher frequencies of vibration as they ascend, have differing functions, and are beyond the range of physical sense perception:

> Different schools of thought refer to these energy bodies by different names. One common system of nomenclature refers to the first four as the etheric body; the astral, or emotional body; the mental body, and the causal, or intuitive body.... As their names suggest, ...three bodies are related to emotional, mental and intuitive processes. Virtually no one agrees on what to call the remaining three bodies, although it is commonly agreed that they have to do with the soul and higher spiritual functioning.[57]

Here, we will more fully describe the functions of each of these 7 human energy fields in order to elucidate the mental attributes of intellect, emotion and will on both the physical and spiritual planes of human existence: "Each frequency level of energy penetrates through the physical body and extends outward from the skin. ... Each level extends out from the skin several

---

[55] Ibid., 39.
[56] Ibid., 7-8.
[57] Talbot, *The Holographic Universe*, 168-69.

inches farther than the one within it of lower frequency."[58]

· Through the first energy level, we experience our five physical senses as well as pleasure and pain. This level is the template for our physical body.

· The second energy level is associated with feelings or emotions we have about ourselves.

· The third energy level is associated with our mental or rational world.

· The fourth level of the human energy field deals with our relationships and how we interact with people, animals, plants, inanimate objects and the universe as a whole. In this field are all of our feelings about others.

· The fifth level is that of divine will where the desire of the Divine in relationship to our individual lives connects to us.

· The sixth level is the level of our divine love. This level is experienced as spiritual love, joy, elation, and bliss.

· The seventh level is the level of divine mind. It has strong golden lines of energy that are interwoven to form all the components of our physical body. It prevents energy leakage from the field as well as penetration by unhealthy energies from outside. It holds the entire human energy field together. Human beings are meant to connect to divine mind in order to experience serenity and our perfected nature.[59]

The first three human energy field (HEF) levels are the mental faculties, that is, will, emotion, and intellect—both rational and intuitive, which are related to our physical self. The fifth, sixth and seventh energy levels are the mental faculties of divine will, emotion, and intellect which are related to our spiritual or higher self. The fourth energy level acts as an emotional bridge between the mind and body of our spiritual self.

The core of our being is designed to be connected to God and we are unique, individual manifestations of God. The human energy fields imbue us with our emotional nature, rationality and intuitiveness (intellect), and willfulness. They also imbue us with desires for self-acceptance, loving relationships, spiritual ecstasy, and connection with divine mind. To reach our full human potential, we need wonderful physical sensations, self-acceptance, harmony of our rational and intuitive minds, loving relationships with others, a commitment to practice the truth, as well as

---

[58] Barbara Brennan, *Light Emerging: The Journey of Personal Healing* (New York: Bantam Books, 1993), 19.
[59] Barbara Brennan, *Light Emerging, passim,* 20-26.

divine love (characterized as unconditional love), and a connection with divine mind.[60]

Energy healers recognize that human beings have what is called a higher and lower self. According to Barbara Brennan,

> [t]he major difference between the higher self (and) lower self...is found in the foundation of underlying intent upon which each is based, and in the quality of energy present in any interaction that results from the underlying intent. The intention of the higher self is for truth, communion, respect, individuality, clear self-awareness, and union with the creator. Our lower self is the part of us that has forgotten who we are. It is the part of our psyche that believes in a separated, negative world and acts accordingly. ... It cannot care both about itself and about another because of its world of separation. ... The intention of the lower self is to maintain separation and to do anything it wants to do, and to not feel pain.[61]

The mental energy field (the third field) is the director of our conscious life. "This means that we can either shut off the higher flow and be ego-centered, allowing little of the higher energies to influence us, or we can receive direction from the Divine, and use that inspiration to guide our conscious lives."[62] Thus, our free will to choose our path in life resides in our mental energy field.

4) Definition of mental health and mental illness

When the human energy fields are in a healthy state, that is, clear, charged, balanced, and synchronized, a person feels "self-accepting, safe, appropriate, and ha(s) personal power."[63] This, then, would be the HEF definition of mental health.

From the HEF perspective, disease—whether physical or mental---is the result of distortions in our consciousness which block our divine essence from flowing through our 7 energy levels into our physical body. In other words, our conscious or unconscious intentions expressed through our thoughts, feelings, and actions, are primary factors which determine our

---

[60] Barbara Brennan, *Light Emerging*, passim 19-26.
[61] Ibid., 8-9.
[62] Barbara Martin and Dimitri Moraitis, *Change Your Aura Change Your Life: A Step-by-Step Guide to Unfolding Your Spiritual Power* (Sunland, CA: WisdomLight Books, 2003), 26.
[63] Brennan, *Light Emerging*, 22.

state of physical or mental health.[64] Thus, if our intentions are always loving and giving, our consciousness will be aligned with our divine essence and we will be healthy. However, if, for instance, our intentions are habitually selfish and greedy, we will block the flow of our divine essence and our energy fields will become dirty, undercharged, stagnant, and imbalanced. (This unhealthy state of the human energy field is sometimes referred to as a devolved aura as opposed to an enlightened aura.) As Barbara Brennan expresses it: "We find that wherever the illness is in the body is where we have not allowed the deeper divine self to express itself."[65]

Why don't we allow the deeper divine self to express itself? One reason is that we automatically try not to feel the pain caused by experiences of not receiving the unconditional love that we naturally expect. But we are actually stopping the flow of energy that contains the pain. This creates a blockage that becomes frozen energy-consciousness. Many such blockages are attracted to each other by their similar energy and can coagulate to form what Barbara Brennan calls frozen psychic time conglomerates. Energy healers generally believe that humans have past lives which can also contribute blockages to our present frozen psychic time conglomerates. Unfortunately, this habitual pain avoidance has the effect of walling off the deeper part of ourselves which is our divine essence.[66] This frozen energy-consciousness can be thawed out through energy healing.

Another reason is proposed by Barbara Brennan:

> The origin of pain, from my perspective, ...comes from the belief that each of us is separate; separate from everyone else and separate from God. Many of us believe that in order to be an individual, we must be separate. As a result, we separate ourselves from everything, including our own families, friends, groups, nations, and the earth. This belief in separation is experienced as fear, and out of fear, all other negative emotions arise. Once we have created these negative emotions, we separate ourselves from them. This process of separating goes on creating more pain and illusion until the negative feedback loop is broken or reversed.... The key is love and connectedness to all that there is (which is one of the premises of holism). Love is the experience of being connected to God and to everything else.[67]

---

[64] Ibid.
[65] Brennan, *Light Emerging*, 133.
[66] Ibid., *passim*, 5-7.
[67] Brennan, *Light Emerging*, 7.

5) The influence of family and environment on mental health

Energy healers can perceive with their higher sense perception how each individual's energy fields affect those whom they are relating to. Too often it is in negative ways. Barbara Brennan explains:

> We...have habitual negative ways of interacting and manipulating each other through our fields. We usually do this out of fear and ignorance. We usually are not consciously aware that we are doing it. ... When we don't learn how to handle somebody's negative energetic actions in a positive healing way, a negative feedback loop can start. Each person may escalate defensive distortion until imagination and projection completely take over. In such cases, very painful damaging interactions can result. This happens on the personal level, between two people; it happens between groups of people; and it happens between nations, many times resulting in war. If we learn to prevent it on the personal level, we will eventually know how to prevent it on the national level.[68]

She explains further how our energy fields interact with the natural environment:

> We have become more and more disconnected from the earth, and it shows everywhere on the planet as disease and natural disasters. When nature is not disrupted, it stays in balance with the broad-scale whole earth energies. The energies of nature charge the auric field and put it into balance with its surroundings. In undisturbed, natural settings, we find our natural synchronicity with the planet's energies. ... Spending several hours every week in an unspoiled setting reestablishes a balance between your auric field and earth energies. This is necessary for full health.[69]

6) The approach for mental health maintenance

Our human energy fields clearly show how our thoughts, feelings and relationships either promote health or cause illness. Learning how to consciously manipulate these fields allows us to

---

[68] Brennan, *Light Emerging*, 203-4.
[69] Ibid., 106.

balance and harmonize all our energy levels in order to maintain our mental as well as physical health.

First, we need to be aware of the energy source that sustains us. Energy healer, Barbara Martin calls the energy that propels the life force of God throughout the universe Spiritual or Divine Light:

> [T]here has to be power that sends the love of God, the peace of God, the wisdom of God...to each of us. ... Spiritual light is part of the divine radiations that emanate from the very heart and mind of God. It is this energy that sustains all life and is he power behind all activities, physical and spiritual. ... Without this energetic onduit, we would have no means of receiving anything from God. ...[I]t enerates the spiritual power necessary to create whatever it is you are focusing your attention on.[70]

In order to maintain mental health from an energy healing perspective, it is also necessary for our consciousness to be connected to the present moment, to our physical body, and to the Earth. Energy healer, Karla McLaren calls this "being grounded."

> Anything that brings you back to the present and back to a sense of pleasure and release is grounding. People who are not grounded tend to be unfocused, unsettled, stress-filled and stressful, and heavily invested in controlling everything around them. People who are naturally grounded are generally earthy, centered, and at home in their bodies. The act of grounding tends to center and focus people, because it calms their body down and creates a warm and peaceful place in which to live. Controlling others becomes unnecessary, because grounding gives the body a way to control itself, release pent-up energy and emotions, and cleanse itself on a moment-by-moment basis. People can connect with their bodies and the Earth in many ways: through touch and body work, through eating, through being out in nature or in water, through contact with animals, and through healthy sex.[71]

7) The treatment approach for mental illness

---

[70] Barbara Martin, *Change Your Aura, Change Your Life*, 4-5.
[71] Karla McLaren, *Your Aura & Your Chakras: the Owner's Manual* (Boston: Weiser Books, 1998, 14-15.

Due to both internal and external stresses, most people's mental, emotional, and spiritual states are unhealthy and need changing. These psychological states can be seen by energy healers as imbalanced energy fields. There are two main treatment approaches used by energy healers to balance the fields: First, manipulation of the patient's energy fields with the energy emanating from the healer's hands and second, teaching patients how to heal themselves using various thought processes including self-inventory, meditation, affirmations, and visualizations.

With the energy manipulation approach, the healer directs healing energy from the universal energy field into the patient's energy system in order to realign, charge, and repair blocked or disturbed energy flow. At the same time, the healer is helping the patient connect to their own creative force and core consciousness. The healer uses HSP or higher sense perception and intuition to perceive the patient's energy fields. With HSP, the healer can ascertain psychological problems, childhood traumas, dietary, vitamin, and mineral deficiencies, as well as the beliefs of the patient that hold energy imbalances in place. Sometimes healers will seek guidance about their patients from spiritual beings who are believed to be guardian angels or other spirit guides. The objective is to not only help patients find the cause of their illness but to help them understand how they themselves are the cause of their illness. [72] Energy healers understand that love can heal anything. "Healers not only work from a place of love, they teach patients to love themselves." [73]

Besides checking for psychic injuries and nutritional imbalances with the assistance of an energy healer, teaching mentally disturbed people to ground, center, meditate, and heal their energy fields and energy intake organs (chakras) is invaluable. [74] This is done through what Barbara Martin calls light work. A meditation technique is employed for drawing light from our spiritual reservoir into our energy fields. It involves deciding what we want the light to do for us, drawing the light into our energy fields and applying the light to effect the change that we desire. A recommended preliminary step, for those who live an habitually unexamined life, is to do a personal inventory of one's strengths and weaknesses in order to recognize parts of oneself that need improvement. Energy healers understand that we create our own world through our thoughts, desires, and emotions. Individuals cannot progress towards maturity by assigning blame for their troubles to others or external circumstances. Instead of asking ourselves the

---

[72] Brennan, *Light Emerging, passim* 58-64.
[73] Ibid., 61.
[74] McLaren, *Your Auras & Your Chakras*, 274.

question, "Why is this happening to me?" we need to ask, "What did I do to create this situation?" The recommended categories for one's "strengths and weaknesses list" include thoughts, emotions, personal affairs, relationships, career, and finances. The weakness that stands out the most is a good starting place to focus on when meditating and drawing light into one's energy field.[75]

In the case of more severe mental illnesses, Karla McLaren advises that "[d]rug therapies and institutionalization may be necessary at times, but once the symptoms have calmed down a bit, ...competent spiritual grounding may help such people explore and heal (through aura healing and chakra alignment) whatever it was that caused them to leave the 'normal' world in the first place."[76]

8) The goal of therapy/counseling/healing

With the energy healing perspective, the goal is to balance and synchronize all 7 of the human energy fields so that a person feels "self-accepting, safe, appropriate, and ha(s) personal power." When this is realized, the rational and intuitive aspects of the mind, as well as the emotion, and will are interacting harmoniously. Energy healers strive to connect their patients to the universal God and to the individual God within so that they can be completely safe and free.

9) Qualifications or attributes of the therapist/counselor/healer

Energy healers are trained in the following areas: They do exercises in order to increase the sensitivity of their senses so that they can feel, hear, see and intuit information about the human energy fields. They must learn how to work with the energy fields in order to heal them. They must also study human anatomy, physiology, psychology, illness, and the ethics of healer-ship.[77] And finally, they are adherents of the holism perspective.

10) Summary of the Human Energy Field / Holism model of mental health and illness:

---

[75] Martin and Moraitis, *Change Your Aura, Change Your Life, passim* 53-55.
[76] McLaren, *Your Auras & Your Chakras*, 274.
[77] Brennan, *Light Emerging*, 61.

(1) Explanation of the ideal human being

An ideal human being is an individual manifestation of God having innate desires for self-acceptance, loving relationships, and connection with God. Such a person's energy fields are clear, balanced and synchronized.

(2) The relationship between the mind and body

The human mind and body have a cause and effect relationship.

(3) The structure of the mind and human nature

The human mind or consciousness is located in the 7 human energy fields which surround and penetrate the physical body. These fields contain the attributes of emotion, intellect and will. The view of human nature is that human beings are individual manifestations of God with emotion, intellect, and will having innate desires for self- acceptance, loving relationships, and connection with God. People have a higher and lower self related to their intention for either connectedness or separation.

(4) Definition of mental health and mental illness

The definition of mental health is balanced and synchronized human energy fields which generate feelings of self-acceptance, safety, appropriateness, and personal power. Mental illness is seen as distortions in our human energy fields which block our divine essence from flowing through them. These distortions are created by selfish intentions, pain avoidance, and/or the erroneous belief that to be an individual, one must be separate from others. Energy blockages can also originate from past lives, not only one's present life. (Most energy healers believe in reincarnation.)

(5) The influence of family and environment on mental health

We...have habitual negative ways of interacting and manipulating each other through our fields. If we learn to prevent it on the personal level, we will eventually know how to prevent it on the national level. We have become more and more disconnected from the earth, and it shows everywhere on the planet as disease and natural disasters. In undisturbed, natural settings, we find our natural synchronicity with the planet's energies.

(6) The approach for mental health maintenance

Mental health can be maintained by learning to consciously balance and harmonize our human energy fields. Also, by staying grounded, that is, by staying connected to the present, one's body, and the Earth.

(7) The treatment approach for mental illness

There are two main modalities for treating mental disorders: A trained energy healer can manipulate a patient's energy fields with the energy emanating from his or her hands. Individuals can heal themselves by learning to direct positive light energy into their energy field through meditation, affirmation, and visualization.

(8) The goal of therapy/counseling/healing

The goal is to balance and synchronize all 7 of the human energy fields so that a person feels self-accepting, safe, appropriate, and has personal power.

(9) Qualifications or attributes of the therapist/counselor/healer

Healers have developed higher sense perception and are trained in healing techniques for the human energy fields. They also have knowledge of human physiology, psychology, and ethics and believe in the holism perspective of health and illness.

The human energy field model understands that the force of God's love, which is referred to as divine essence, has been distorted and blocked which leads to both physical and mental illness. However, the root cause of this distortion and blockage is not clarified. Therefore, this model cannot provide an ultimate solution for mental illness.

CHAPTER II   THE UNIFICATION THOUGHT MODEL: A HOLISTIC AND
               COMPREHENSIVE PERSPECTIVE

1. Explanation of the ideal human being

Unification Thought (UT) is a systematic theistic philosophy based on revelation received by the Rev. Dr. Sun Myung Moon (Father Moon). UT asserts that all existing beings in the cosmos were designed to exist since their creation based upon the motive and purpose originating from God, the Creator:

> With heart as the motive, God created human beings and all things as His object partners of love.[78] Heart is the emotional impulse to seek joy through love... [A]ll phenomena...are supported and permeated by the impulse of love.[79] ...[T]he force of love, as well as physical force (energy), is at work among all things of the universe.[80]

Certain principles are operating throughout the cosmos so that God's purpose for love and joy can be realized (which UT refers to as the Law of the Universe or the Way of Heaven).[81] God created all existing beings to be in a cause and effect relationship with Him, resembling His dual characteristics of internal nature (heart of love) and external form (energy) as well as yin and yang (that is, masculinity and femininity in human beings). The dual characteristics of all existing beings interact in a subject (initiating) and object (responding) relationship through give and receive action (GRA) which is prompted by God's universal prime energy. Give and receive action is designed to have the characteristics of purposefulness, order, position and harmony so that the purpose of God's creation can be fulfilled. A four position foundation (FPF) for life and the realization of goodness is formed when the dual characteristics of an entity have harmonious interaction and form a union centered upon God.[82]

---

78 Unification Thought Institute (UTI), *New Essentials of Unification Thought; Head-Wing Thought*. (Bridgeport, CT: The Research Institute of the Integration of World Thought, 2006), 24.

79 UTI, *New Essentials of Unification Thought, 32.*

80 Ibid., 27.

81 Ibid., 147-48.

82 The Holy Spirit Association for the Unification of World Christianity, *Exposition of the Divine Principle* (New York: H.S.A.-U.W.C., revised edition, 2006), 25.

An ideal human being is fundamentally the harmonized oneness of the dual characteristics of mind in the subject position and body in the object position centered upon God's heart and the Way of Heaven. An ideal human being is an "individual four position foundation" of goodness and is a person with a loving character who lives according to the Way of Heaven, thus returning joy to God by resembling His nature.[83]

2. The ideal relationship between the mind and the body

The human mind and body have a cause and effect relationship between an internal nature and external form. The body follows the direction of the mind through give and receive action. An individual whose mind is centered upon God's motivation of heart and whose body completely and continually follows the mind's direction is a mature individual with good character.

Unification Thought asserts that mind and body, or spirit and matter, share common elements that are able to interact. The mind is our individual consciousness made up of energy and our body, which is our material aspect, also has some level of consciousness even down to the cellular level.[84]

3. The original, ideal structure of the mind and human nature

The internal nature of the cosmos is the incorporeal spirit world and its external form is the physical world. God created human beings as the model for the cosmos. Thus, human beings have both a spirit body centered upon a spirit mind as well as a physical body centered upon a physical mind. The human spirit self is meant to develop its ability to love during the physical lifetime through the fulfillment of human responsibility and then go on to exist for eternity in the realm of God's love in the spirit world (Heaven).[85]

According to Unification Thought:

The human mind consists of the spirit mind and physical mind. The

---

[83] UTI, *New Essentials of Unification Thought*, 179-80.
[84] Ibid., 9-10.
[85] H.S.A.-U.W.C., *Exposition of the Divine Principle*, 49.

relationship between these two minds is like that between internal nature and external form. When they become one through give and receive action with God as their center, they form a united functioning entity which guides the spirit self and physical self to become harmonious and progress toward the purpose of creation.[86]

The function of the spirit mind is to guide us in pursuit of a life of truth, goodness, beauty, and love, namely, a life of value...a life of love in which one lives for the sake of the family,...nation, humankind, and ultimately for God. In contrast, the function of the physical mind is to guide us in pursuit of a life of food, clothing, shelter, and sex, namely, a material life. Material life is a life centered on the individual.[87]

When the relationship between the two minds is harmonious, certain elements are exchanged between the human spirit self and physical self:

When the physical mind obeys the spirit mind and the physical self acts according to the good purpose of the spirit mind, the physical self receives living spirit elements from the spirit self and becomes wholesome. In return, the physical self provides good vitality elements to the spirit self, which enables the spirit self to grow properly in the direction of goodness.[88]

In (the function of) cognition, the spirit mind makes a judgment of value, while the physical mind manages sensation, and they jointly engage in the work of memory.[89]

As well, both the spirit mind and the physical mind have the attributes of intellect, emotion, and will. "The physical mind has an instinctive level of intellect, emotion and will. The intellect, emotion and will of the spirit mind is creative and developmental.... ...The spirit mind thinks of, and reflects upon, oneself; namely, it possesses self-consciousness."[90] "When the give and receive action between intellect, emotion, and will is balanced, it is guided by the love that

---

[86] Ibid., 50.
[87] UTI, *New Essentials of Unification Thought*, 156.
[88] H.S.A.-U.W.C., *Exposition of the Divine Principle*, 48.
[89] UTI, *New Essentials of Unification Thought*, 418.
[90] Ibid., 59.

resides at the center of our being."[91]

UT recognizes and explains the role of the conscience as follows:

> The conscience is that faculty of the human mind which...always directs us toward what we think is good. The original mind is that faculty of the human mind which pursues absolute goodness. It relates to the conscience as internal nature to external form.[92]

The original mind is actually the harmonized oneness of the spirit mind and the physical mind, when they have the originally intended give and receive action. Thus, human nature is meant to pursue a life expressing truth, beauty, goodness and unselfish love. It is the nature to return joy to God according to the desires of the original mind.

4. Definition of mental health and mental illness

From the UT perspective, mental health is realized when human beings establish an individual four position foundation centered on God's heart and the Way of Heaven. This is when there is a harmonious relationship of the spirit mind and physical mind. Then the attributes of intellect, emotion, and will function in a balanced way and the desires to express truth, beauty, goodness, and unselfish love can be actualized. In other words, an ideal human being is a mentally healthy human being and a mentally healthy human being is an ideal human being. Such a person has a calm, peaceful, and loving state of mind.

Unification Thought (UT) explains that the original instruction given by God to His children, "be fruitful and multiply, and ...have dominion...." (Genesis 1:28), was for the purpose of realizing His ideal for human beings and the creation. Once realized, all relationships beginning with the relationship of the human spirit mind and physical mind would be healthy, that is, balanced and harmonious. In UT, this instruction of God to his first son and daughter is called the three great blessings. In other words, individuals are to nurture their character to resemble God's (individual four position foundation) and then, when mature, receive God's blessing in marriage. A Godly husband and wife who relate harmoniously are to become the

---

[91] Robert and Janice Maddox, *Deep Origin Healing and the Origin of Personality Distortion*, (U.S.A.: Maddox Multimedia, 2012). 157.

[92] H.S.A.-U.W.C., *Exposition of the Divine Principle*, 50.

complete reflection of God's fatherly and motherly nature of unconditional, sacrificial (true) love. Then they are to bear children and exemplify for them God's way of true love. This is the family four position foundation which fulfills the instruction "to multiply." God intended that the family be the school of love that teaches its members how to relate to the wider community and world in such a way that His love circulates well. Godly families are to care for the natural world and creatively use it to make a comfortable and even more beautiful living environment. This is the four position foundation of dominion in which human beings relate harmoniously with all created beings.

Essentially, we are intended by God to resonate with His heart. We are meant to grow through our family relationships and to come to love as God loves, with an unconditional heart to love and care for others and the natural world as a true parent. As God's children, resembling His nature, we are to maintain our proper position and fulfill our God-given responsibility by cultivating what UT calls "connected-being consciousness" or "dual purposes."[93] This means that we participate in various relationships in our daily life, as a child, sibling, spouse, parent, leader, teacher, etc.. In some relationships we are in the subject position meant to give care and concern to those who we are leading as an elder sibling, spouse, parent, teacher, or leader. In other relationships we are in the object position meant to return filial piety, obedience, or loyalty to our parent, teacher, or leader respectively. In this way we maintain orderly, healthy relationships and the force of love coming from God circulates well. By so doing, we realize our spiritual purpose and desire by multiplying, through relationships in our family and society, truth, beauty, goodness and true love.[94]

Attitudes and behaviors of truth, beauty, and goodness include taking responsibility, gratitude, appreciation, respect for self and others, honesty, empathy, patience, loyalty, filial piety, chastity, fidelity, humility, obedience, kindness, compassion, generosity, self-reflection, and repentance.

God also endowed His children with free will, expecting that we freely respond to His love and guidance and thus be the origin of eternal joy and happiness. Thus, the original ideal for human nature serves as a standard and goal for the achievement and maintenance of mental health.

---

[93] UTI, *New Essentials of Unification Thought*, 176.
[94] Ibid.

Unification Thought defines mental illness as the condition of the human mind that has not realized the individual four position foundation. In other words, where the desires of the spirit mind and physical mind are not harmonized centered upon God's love and the Way of Heaven but are instead in conflict and separated from God. The inner contradiction that all human beings experience is evidence that humankind is suffering from a collective mental illness! This was not intended by God. Therefore, there has to be a beginning point of this tragic circumstance in human history.

1) The Root Cause of Mental Illness

From the Unification Thought perspective, the separation of our original human ancestors from God, and the consequent realization of a "fallen" human nature, in contradistinction to an original ideal human nature, is the root cause of mental illness. Consequently, all of humankind, other existing beings, and God Himself---who is our loving parent---have experienced continual pain, suffering, and misery.

The UT perspective of the root cause of mental illness is derived from the explanation of the motivation and process of the human fall revealed to Father Moon which can be found in the second section of the second chapter of his fundamental teaching, The Divine Principle.[95] Within this section there is a full exposition of the original deviation from the true love relationships which God intended. From the story of the "eating of the fruit" by Lucifer the Archangel, Eve, and Adam in the Garden of Eden, it is possible to deduce the origin of dysfunctional (false) love relationships. In particular, Divine Principle provides insights about dysfunction within the human personality and human relationships which was inherited through the blood lineage. These insights have implications for better understanding mental health, mental illness, and improving the efficacy of the therapeutic/healing approach. And, they are able to resolve some of the limitations in the models being considered in this study.

Here, we briefly summarize the Divine Principle explanation: After God created the cosmos with the assistance of the angels, led by the Archangel Lucifer, He created the first male and female human beings, Adam and Eve, in an immature physical and spiritual state. Lucifer's responsibility was, in the position of a servant, to guide and care for Adam and Eve during the

---

[95] H.S.A.-U.W.C., *Exposition of the Divine Principle*, 62-65.

time of their growth to maturity. Before their creation, Lucifer had been the direct recipient of God's love. Once God had created his beloved son and daughter, Lucifer felt a lack of love and an envious heart toward Adam. He nurtured a grudge in his heart which led him to seduce Eve to disobey the commandment which God gave to Adam and Eve, "not to eat of the fruit of the Tree of the Knowledge of Good and Evil." The commandment to "not eat of the fruit" meant to not have a sexual relationship until the time when God could give permission for a mature Adam and a mature Eve to become husband and wife as the full reflection of God's loving nature. Lucifer succeeded in drawing Eve into an illicit sexual relationship between their spiritual bodies. Afterwards, Eve felt conscience-stricken and desired to return to her proper position as Adam's intended wife. With this motivation she seduced Adam into a sexual relationship with her before the time of their maturity. Being immature, they were not ready to consummate their relationship as husband and wife. Through this process, the Archangel, Eve, and Adam failed to keep God's commandment and viewpoint, left their proper positions, and reversed the proper order of dominion from God, children and servant to the servant dominating God's children and their forsaking of God. This was the origin and beginning of the multiplication of unrighteousness or evil which was never intended by God. It was fundamentally the failure of the responsibility given by God to Adam and Eve during their growing period before they had fulfilled the 1st blessing of maturity of heart centered on God's true love. Tragically, Adam and Eve became bound in blood ties with Lucifer through their sexual deviation and thus, the tendencies of their deviation from God were passed down from generation to generation through the blood lineage until now. UT refers to these tendencies as fallen nature. So, instead of realizing our originally intended ideal nature, we inherited the fallen tendencies as follows:

original "ideal" human nature:	fallen nature:
* keep God's viewpoint	* fail to keep God's viewpoint
* keep one's proper position	* leave one's proper position
* keep one's proper dominion	* reverse one's proper dominion
* multiply goodness	* multiply evil

2) Consequences of the Deviation of the Original Human Ancestors from God's Purpose for Their Creation:

(1) Satan and fallen humanity

According to the Divine Principle, "Satan is the name given to the Archangel Lucifer after he fell. ... Adam and Eve...while still immature...fell and formed a four position foundation centering on Satan. Consequently, the world has come under Satan's sovereignty."[96] God's purpose of creation has yet to be realized because the ideal of the three great blessings remains unfulfilled.

(2) Inheritance of fallen nature and sin through the blood lineage

When Eve and then Adam united with Lucifer's will in violation of God's commandment "not to eat of the fruit," their original nature became misdirected. Their original, pure desires failed to align with God's point of view and heart and instead, became centered on their own point of view. From this tendency for self-centeredness sprang other fallen tendencies including jealousy, hatred, anger, greed, dishonesty, arrogance, and the potential to fornicate (lustful desire).[97]

Human beings have thus come to have both fallen nature and original nature within their minds and hearts. These two natures contradict each other and are in conflict within each person's mind so that human beings are unable to pursue only truth, beauty, and goodness as directed by their spirit mind and conscience. Instead, the stronger tendency is to act upon the desires of the physical or self-centered mind just as Lucifer, Adam and Eve did in the Garden of Eden. Thus, human beings throughout human history have continually felt dissatisfaction and a lack of fulfillment and happiness. St. Paul testified to this internal contradiction in his own mind in the letter he wrote to the Roman Christian community:

> For I delight in the law of God, in my inmost self, but I see in my members another law at war with the law of my mind and making me captive to the law of sin which dwells in my members. Wretched man that I am! (Romans 7:22-24, RSV)

---

[96] H.S.A.-U.W.C., *Exposition of the Divine Principle*, 68.
[97] Cheongpyeong Heaven and Earth Training Center, "In Search of the True Self" 3rd ed. (Seorak-myeon: Cheongpyeong Training Center, 2007), 52.

Sin is defined by Unification Thought as the violation of our original nature which seeks for truth, beauty and goodness by making a common base and having give and receive action with the tendencies derived from the original deviation (fall) of Adam and Eve. Sin is classified into four categories: the original sin of fornication and adultery, hereditary sin passed on through the blood lineage, collective sin which is committed by a group of people, and personal sin; sin that we commit as individuals.[98] As a result of the deviation of the original human ancestors, our original nature has remained latent within us but has not developed because sin and fallen nature has been multiplied instead.

(3) The inversion of the intended relationship of the spirit mind and the physical mind:

The dual purposes of the human mind became reversed as a result of Adam and Eve's deviation. In other words, the physical mind did not realize it's intended role of responding to the direction of the spirit mind in order to actualize truth, goodness, beauty, and altruistic love. There was a breakdown of the originally intended interaction. This deviation of the relationship of the spirit and physical mind has been passed on from generation to generation as an intergenerational, collective habit that has kept us in a state of selfishness disconnected from our original human nature. However, there remains within us an innate potential for our spirit and physical minds to harmonize and form our original mind. Our conscience, as well, continues to direct us toward goodness although it is hindered by our ignorance of the truth.

(4) The origin of dysfunction in family relationships

God's ideal of the three great blessings was not realized in the original human family. The consequence of unrealized original human nature was false love, that is, selfish love which is manipulative, abusive, or neglectful. False love was multiplied and passed on from generation to generation. Thus, dysfunctional relationships have been manifested starting with the

---

[98] HSA-UWC, Exposition of Divine Principle, 72.

misdirected relationship of our spirit mind and physical mind, then between couples, in families, and in society in general.

(5) The origin of psychological trauma

When we experience false expressions of love, psychological pain and trauma is the result. It is sometimes referred to as a psychic or emotional "wound." One might say that humanity has inherited a "collective emotional wound" from the original deviation from God's force of love in the Garden of Eden. As we try to cope with such dysfunctional or completely broken relationships in our lives, we naturally resort to psychological defense mechanisms which are usually triggered unconsciously. This self-defense tendency has the effect of distorting our perceptions of self, others, and God. We become trapped in these distortions and our relationships lose their originally intended joyfulness and meaning.[99] As a result, we may experience low self-regard, feelings of unworthiness, guilt, shame, depression, and neurosis (anxiety), etc.

Instead of God's true love being manifested through our relationships, conflictual and destructive relationships have been actualized in an unceasing and vicious cycle. Thus, negative mental states have been induced such as anger, resentment, hatred, and pessimism, etc. We have come to feel, deep in our hearts, a loneliness like that of an orphan who lacks the sacrificial and unconditional love of parents. Thus, we struggle to feel any value to our existence, a struggle which provokes an unstable mental state characterized by dissatisfaction, frustration, anxiety, despair, and other negative and self-destructive feelings.

(6) Negative influence from spirit persons in the Spiritual World

UT asserts that our spirit self continues to exist in the spiritual realm eternally after the death of our physical body.[100] Every person who ever lived on Earth exists eternally as a spirit mind and body with memories of their physical lifetime. If they kept strong resentment as a result of mistreatment by others, those spirit persons seek to take revenge on the descendants of

---

[99] Robert and Janice Maddox, *Deep Origin Healing and the Origin of Personality Distortion*, (U.S.A.: Maddox Multimedia, 2001), xxxii.
[100] H.S.A.-U.W.C., *Exposition of the Divine Principle*, 46.

47

their tormentors, thus causing accidents, as well as physical or mental illness. In extreme cases, spirit persons try to completely dominate the spirit of a person on earth. This is known as spirit possession. [101] Mrs. Hyo-nam Kim, the spiritual leader of the Unification movement's Cheongpyeong Training Center in South Korea explains this phenomenon:

> In our bodies are evil spirits with resentment and hatred. These are filling us up fully. These evil spirits came to us to release their resentment and grudge. As they were harmed by our ancestors, they want to hurt us, but even more. Of all the diseases and problems we suffer, 90% are spiritual in nature. ... In our bodies, evil spirits are dominating and controlling our hearts and minds. Without removing them, we cannot remove fallen nature. ... Without removing evil spirits from the physical body, we cannot be happy or at peace. [102]

Furthermore, we inherit not only physical traits, but character traits as well from our ancestors. Our own thoughts and feelings are influenced by our ancestors through their give and receive action with our minds throughout our physical lifetime. We also hold within us the memory of trauma experienced by our own lineage as well as those spirit persons who are trying to harm us. Thus, torment and oppression by evil, resentful spirit person's is an underlying cause of mental illness. [103]

(7) The fundamental purpose of religion to restore the intended relationship of our spirit and physical minds.

God has raised up founders of various religions in order to guide His children, who have developed diverse cultures over the centuries, back to their original nature which resonates with and resembles His own divine nature. All the major religions of the world have put emphasis on denying the self-centered mind in order to correct the reversed relationship of the spirit and physical minds. [104]

---

[101] For an in-depth discussion of spirit possession, refer to the book, *The Unquiet Dead* by psychiatrist Edith Fiore.
[102] Hyo-nam Kim (Daemonim), speech given at Cheongpyeong Training Center, July 14, 2012.
[103] For meticulously documented evidence of spirit attachment to earthly people, refer to the book, *Remarkable Healings; A Psychiatrist Discovers Unsuspected Roots of Mental and Physical Illness* by Shakuntala Modi, M.D.
[104] Walsh, *World Scripture*, 896.

5. The influence of family and environment on mental health

If God's ideal of the three great blessings had been fulfilled beginning in Adam's family, human beings would have manifested their original nature of goodness and mental health would have been easy to maintain. That is because children would be able to grow to maturity raised by true parents who exemplify altruistic, sacrificial, and unconditional love. Within a God-centered family human beings can experience the realms of children's love for parents, sibling love, love of husband and wife, and love of parents. The family is meant to be the school of true love that teaches norms based on the Way of Heaven for relating to others in the greater society as well as with the natural world. Experiencing harmony with nature is conducive to mental health as well. But because Satan came to dominate the four position foundations of the individual, family, and all things, false love, as well as false beliefs and norms have multiplied from generation to generation which has inevitably led to the collective mental illness of humankind in the form of fallen nature and sin.

6. The approach for maintenance of mental health

Father Moon teaches that there are eight necessary elements for achieving and maintaining mental health:

1) devotional time for studying God's word at the beginning of each day
2) mind and body unity practice and self-reflection through occasional training sessions away from home
3) holding occasional "mental" cultural festivals when mind and body unity practices such as meditation, martial arts, yoga, tai chi, tea ceremonies, etc., can be experienced and celebrated
4) pure artistic activity which aids a healthy emotional state
5) wholesome hobby activity with family and friends
6) regular physical exercise which supports healthy brain function
7) balanced and nutritious eating habits

8) holistic medical treatment.[105]

Particularly, daily study of God's word which provides guidance concerning the meaning and purpose of human existence as well as norms for achieving that purpose (which are the three great blessings) is nourishment for the spirit mind.

7. The treatment approach for mental illness

1) Dr. Yuji Ootomo's Counseling approach

Dr. Yuji Ootomo is a practicing clinical psychologist who has been pioneering the integration of mainstream psychotherapy and counseling with the Unification Thought perspective. Unification Thought asserts that religion, which has sought to overcome our internal, spiritual ignorance, and science, which has sought to overcome our ignorance of the physical world, should unite in an integrated undertaking and progress in full consonance. Only in this way, can any and all human problems be solved.[106] This is because human beings have both a spiritual aspect and a physical aspect which are meant to relate in harmonious oneness in order to achieve and maintain physical and mental health as well as to fulfill their God-given purpose.

Dr. Ootomo has stated that, "Because of this new way of counseling, more problems are being solved than were solved previously (in my practice). It proves to be more effective than conventional counseling...since it is based on the universal truth of Father's teachings (Father Moon)."[107]

Here we will summarize his basic insights both in theory and in practice. First, he discusses the background of problems of the mind: Although there are many types of mental disorders, Dr. Ootomo has identified two elements which all these disorders have in common; they are anxiety and anger. He defines anxiety as a conviction that something bad might happen which leads to restlessness but with an inability to do anything about it. He defines anger as a

---

[105] Do Young Yoon. *True Father on Mental Health (research in progress): chapter 4, How to Achieve Mental Health.* (Seorak-myeon: Cheongshim Graduate School of Theology, 2009), 50.

[106] H.S.A.-U.W.C., *Exposition of the Divine Principle,* 3.

[107] Yuji Ootomo, *Completed Testament Pastoral Counseling: The Psychology of Tribal Witnessing,* lecture series, 2011, 3.

destructive impulse from which nothing good can result. Mentally ill people typically cannot see things objectively. For instance, depressed people are very pessimistic. This comes from an anxious state of mind. Also, mentally ill people typically cannot behave rationally or appropriately. This is the result of an angry mental state.[108]

After expressing anger, we feel disgusted with ourselves and it stimulates anxiety and anger in others. It becomes a vicious cycle of unresolved issues which are passed on from generation to generation. Dr. Ootomo asserts that without making an effort to change the most fundamental relationship of parent and child, there can be no resolution of this vicious cycle of anxiety and anger. It is a hereditary problem which can be traced all the way back to Adam's family.

Dr. Ootomo explains that, as a result of the motive and process of Adam and Eve's deviation from God's love and will, their family became the first dysfunctional family full of domestic violence and child abuse. The first fratricide (murder of a sibling) took place when their elder son Cain killed his younger brother Abel. How did this come about? Lucifer's motive to seduce Eve came from his feeling of a lack of love. Once Adam and Eve were created and God began to focus His love and attention towards them, Lucifer's self respect was hurt. He felt lonely and anxious about his existence which developed into resentment and anger. He desired Eve but not with a pure heart which wants to give joy and happiness to another. Instead, there was the destructive impulse of anger which he gave to Eve. Through the process of their improper sexual relationships, Adam and Eve inherited intense anxiety and anger from Lucifer. As a result, their original human nature to desire to express truth, beauty and goodness was severely damaged. They became confused with no vision or hope for the future. Their first son Cain likely experienced neglect and abuse due to his parents' anxiety and anger. Parental anger destroys a child's heart, character, and dignity. Once Abel was born, it is likely that Adam and Eve did not relate to Cain and Abel equally. Cain probably felt jealous of Abel, particularly when Abel's sacrificial offering was accepted but his was not. Adam, Eve, and Abel should have understood Cain's feelings and comforted him. Evidently, no one comforted him because he ultimately expressed his pent up anxiety and anger by killing his brother. Therefore, the anxiety and anger in our families is the same as in Adam's family. From this realization we can understand that the problems of the mind are historical and hereditary.

---

[108] Ootomo, *Completed Testament Age Pastoral Counseling*, passim 7-9.

Underlying anxiety and anger is a feeling of loneliness. The ultimate anxiety which all human beings experience is the loneliness of being disconnected from God's love which is meant to flow to us through our parent-child relationship. Even though we have all inherited a deviated, fallen nature through our blood lineage, our original human nature is still latent within us, albeit undeveloped, so that we always desire a connection of heart with God and parents who love us with an unconditional and sacrificial heart.[109]

Practically speaking, how can problems of the mind be overcome? The key is in understanding the power of give and receive action. A common base is formed and power is generated when counterparts are similar. Therefore, if one person is expressing original nature towards another, it will stimulate feelings of original nature in the other person rather than fallen nature. So, if fallen nature is being expressed, it is important not to return fallen nature but to respond with original nature. If any small act of thoughtfulness for the other is repeated, the feelings of original nature will grow in the recipient and fallen nature will decrease. One need only express simple words such as "thank you" and "I'm sorry" with a motive and feeling of original nature.

Dr. Ootomo outlines three necessary steps for overcoming fallen nature in human relationships:

Step 1: distinguish between a person's original nature and fallen nature. He calls this "separating out the trash."

Step 2: make effort to decrease the fallen nature (break bad habits)

Step 3: grow to become a person of good character, that is, original nature without fallen nature. (establish habits of goodness)

In reality, this is quite difficult to accomplish so Dr. Ootomo recommends as a starting point to never get angry. Even if we are victimized by someone, forgive them and act rationally.

The parent-child relationship is a lineal relationship. Therefore, resolving anxiety and anger in the parent-child relationship can lead to resolving anxiety and anger in oneself.

Dr. Ootomo recommends doing a self-inventory by making three written lists:

1. what you can't forgive, starting with your parent-child relationship

2. what you are grateful for in your parent-child relationship

3. what you want to apologize for in your relationship

---

[109] Ibid., passim 20-26.

Original nature is based on love and trust. Someone in a family needs to determine to break the vicious cycle so as not to pass anxiety and anger on to the next generation. Someone has to take responsibility and commit to breaking the cycle by resolving anxiety and anger in the lineage. Starting with the parent-child relationship, the goal is to realize a heart of filial piety towards one's parents which is essentially the desire to give sacrificial love.[110]

2) The new fallen nature/defenses theory and healing approach

Robert and Janice Maddox are an American Unificationist couple who are both Reiki masters and graduates of a 4-year healing science program. They acknowledge the insights within the Divine Principle regarding the origin of our separation from God as the source of both God's and humankind's continual suffering. Together, they have synthesized the biblical account of the deviation of humankind from God with psycho-dynamic principles, energetic dimensions and spiritual laws in order to create a new healing paradigm that they call D.E.E.P. Origin healing. (The acronym stands for Divine energy, emotional process.)[111] Their theory draws comparisons between fallen human natures and the psycho-dynamic personality distortions (FN/defenses), also known as defenses, originally systematized by Dr. Wilhelm Reich, founder of somatic psychology.[112] They see fallen natures as the root energies for these defenses: "We have shown how fallen natures---original broken human patterns---have been imprinted in our hearts, passing through the lineage to reconstitute themselves in each successive generation."[113] Thus, their healing approach deals with the historical root cause of human personality dysfunction. Briefly stated, the correlation they have made between the fallen natures and personality distortions is as follows:

· Failure to see from God's viewpoint created the schizoid personality distortion
· Leaving one's proper position created the oral personality distortion
· Reversing dominion created the psychopath personality distortion
· Multiplying evil created the masochist personality distortion
· Shifting blame to others created the rigid personality distortion

[110] Ibid., passim 41-53.
[111] Robert and Janice Maddox, *Deep Origin Healing*, xvii.
[112] For an in-depth discussion of personality distortions/defenses and how they correlate with fallen nature, refer to Chapter Six in *Deep Origin Healing and the Origin of Personality Distortion.*
[113] Ibid., 188.

In their healing approach, they guide participants to develop the practice of naming their own defenses when they see them, connecting them to the root fallen natures. Then they are encouraged to meditate and pray about what they have uncovered through their process of introspection and self-examination. Keeping a journal is recommended in order to track personal emotional patterns which help to identify one's FN/defenses. It is emphasized that one should remain a neutral, objective observer of one's emotional patterns, similar to the non-judgmental mindfulness practice of Buddhism. Engaging in a physical discipline such as tai chi, yoga, or marital arts is also encouraged. It is an on-going process in which one can surrender the ego through repentance. The process involves the three fundamental steps of self-awareness, disintegration of defenses, and reintegration of one's original mind/higher self, thus establishing healthy thought patterns, habits and behaviors. The goal is personal transformation and ultimately, true freedom.

3) One Mission of the Cheongpyeong Heaven and Earth Training Center: restoring ancestors and spirit persons who negatively influence earthly people

Because all people are influenced by the spirit world, the Cheongpyeong Heaven and Earth Training Center on the shore of Cheongpyeong Lake in South Korea was established in 1995. There, people can liberate and restore vengeful spirits who are attached to them as well as their own fallen ancestors. By doing so, it becomes much easier for fallen people to discover and develop their own true, original nature. As the training center handbook explains:

> ...(R)esentful spirits are truly the cause of our sickness and suffering. Therefore, we are not living the way we desire, and cannot direct ourselves as we want. In other words, we are being driven by some other being, living according to the way these spirits direct us. We need to understand this clearly. ... True Parents...are allowing us to remove these evil and resentful spirits. Thus, we can eliminate the root cause of these problems. We can live with our own true mind. ... Nothing like this exists in the Christian churches or the Buddhist, Confucian or Islamic faiths. It is only here where the Messiah is. ... In the entire human history of mankind, it was only at the time of Jesus, as well as now at this time of the Second Coming, when the angels worked to remove the evil spirits. ... We have inherited what our ancestors have done throughout history. Therefore, we have to have the determination to get rid of all our old

habits and adopt new habits of goodness, which are connected to God and True Parents. ...(I)f you don't get rid of these problems, either you suffer the consequences or you have to leave them all to your children to resolve when you go to the spirit world.[114]

Through participation in the continuously on-going training sessions held there, earthly people can gradually restore their lineage back to the original relationships of true love intended by God. The liberated spirit persons are guided to restore their own original nature through training provided in the spirit world. Once restored, they can work together with their descendants or other receptive earthly people to cooperate in God's work of restoring His original ideal. UT calls this spirit world-physical world cooperation, "returning spirit resurrection."[115] This process removes the base for mental illness caused by the negative influence of resentful and evil spirits and thus opens a healing pathway back to mental health.[116]

4) Restoring our blood lineage back to God's lineage

Father Moon's teaching reveals the necessity for the advent of true parents in human history who come as mediators to engraft fallen humankind back into God's lineage:

> Who is the Savior that is needed by fallen humankind? The Savior should not be in the position of fallen parents, but instead in the position of Adam and Eve who have not fallen. From there, they can...give rebirth to humanity in the position of true parents. Otherwise, human beings can never rise to the position where they would have no connection at all with the original sin.[117]

Father Moon has elucidated the reality of what humankind inherited from the fall of the original human ancestors:

> People in today's world may boast that they are high and important, or

---

[114] Cheongpyeong Heaven and Earth Training Center, "In Search of the True Self" 3rd ed. (Seorak-myeon: Cheongpyeong Training Center, 2007), passim 49-51.

[115] H.S.A.-U.W.C., *Exposition of the Divine Principle*, 144-45.

[116] Cheongpyeong Heaven and Earth Training Center, "In Search of the True Self," 18.

[117] Family Federation for World Peace and Unification, *Cheon Seong Gyeong: Selections from the Speeches of True Parents*, (Seoul: FFWPU, 2006), 1263.

tell you about their academic degrees, but they don't realize that they were misbegotten at birth. They do not know that they were born with the love, life and lineage of Satan, God's enemy. This is a serious problem. Due to the human fall, people have been born from Satan's love, which was passed down to them through their parents. ... For this reason, each of you belongs to the lineage of Satan. In other words, you could say that Satan's blood is running in your veins. Our ancestors made a mistake. Because of this, countless people throughout the course of human history have suffered as a result. Knowing this, we cannot go that same path again. Never again! We paid a ghastly price throughout history for having perpetuated illicit love in the fallen spiritual and physical worlds, with far- reaching consequences for individuals, families, societies, nations and the world. Thus Satan bears his ideal fruit automatically, while God strives to redeem those very men and women and transform them into pure and perfect people of the original vision. ... Since the beginning was wrong, you must return to the original point. ... We need to go back to the origin. As we originated from false parents, we need to return and start anew from true parents. ... It is imperative to inherit God's love, life and lineage afresh. That's why, when you receive the (marriage) Blessing, you undergo a ceremony for Changing your lineage. ... It is like a wonder drug, an antidote, to restore the dead back to life.[118]

The marriage blessing is the salvific ceremony through which the original sin can be forgiven by Father and Mother Moon, the True Parents of Humankind acknowledged by God. Couples who participate in the Marriage Blessing are then able to give birth to children born without original sin.

It is each person's responsibility, however, to remove their inherited, collective and personal sin and fallen nature. In this way, human beings can be restored back into the lineage of God after having been born into the lineage of God's enemy (Satan), the fallen Archangel Lucifer.

8. The goal of therapy/counseling

1) Eliminate fallen nature and 3 kinds of sin

---

[118] Sun Myung Moon, *True Families, Gateway to Heaven,* (New York: HSA-UWC, 2009), 82-83.

In order to solve problems of the mind, fallen nature and three kinds of sin (hereditary, collective, and personal sins) must be resolved. It is the nature inherited through the fall of Adam and Eve which resulted in human separation from God, domination by Satan, and the loss of proper order within the human mind and all relationships involving human beings. It is each individual's responsibility to recognize their sin and fallen nature and strive to break fallen habits of thinking, feeling, and behavior.

2) Develop latent original nature

The desires of the spirit mind to express truth, beauty, and goodness by harmonizing with the physical mind is what is latent within fallen people, unrealized due to the fall when the physical mind began to dominate the spirit mind. Once individuals overcome their ignorance concerning this reality and recognize their true potential, they can strive to not only break bad habits but establish habits of expressing their original nature.

3) Restore one's lineage beginning with the parent/child relationship

Problems of the mind are inherited particularly when anger and resentment remain unresolved in a person's lineage. Also, spirit person's who were harmed by our ancestors want to take revenge upon the descendants of a lineage by causing accidents and both physical and mental problems. Thus, there are two aspects of restoring one's lineage: First, someone in the lineage needs to take responsibility to resolve anger and resentment by showing gratitude, service, repentance and forgiveness first towards one's parents (who are the channel for love to flow to their children) and then towards other living relatives. Resolving difficult relationships with living relatives also heals the hearts of ancestors. The second aspect is to liberate and restore both ancestors and resentful spirit persons attached to earthly persons through participation in the spiritual works of the Cheongpyeong Training Center in South Korea.

4) Ultimately, receive the forgiveness of original sin from the True Parents in order to return to God's blood lineage and be able to give birth to children without original sin

9. Qualifications or attributes of the therapist/counselor/healer

Father Moon has said, in a talk to medical professionals, that "the attitude of the doctor towards the patient and his life should be like a top religionist and never materialistic. ... You have to concentrate, you have to pray deeply. Even western doctors have to be a kind of real Taoist, a real thinker, a real spiritualist. You have to be absolutely unselfish, have an absolutely clear mind. You really have to live like a monk!"[119] This is the basic UT guideline for those who would counsel and treat individuals and families who suffer from dysfunctional relationships due to sin and fallen nature.

10. Summary of the UT model of mental health and mental illness:

(1) Explanation of the ideal human being

An ideal human being is fundamentally the harmonized oneness of the dual characteristics of mind in the subject position and body in the object position centered upon God's heart and the Way of Heaven.

(2) The relationship between the mind and body

The human mind and body have a relationship of cause and effect or internal nature and external form. This is possible because they share common elements which can interact.

(3) The structure of the mind and human nature

The fundamental attributes of the human mind are called the spirit mind and the physical mind. When harmonized through give and take action centered on God, they form the original mind which pursues goodness and emphasizes true love. Human nature is meant to pursue a life expressing truth, beauty, goodness and unselfish love. It is the nature to return joy to God according to the desires of the original mind.

(4) Definition of mental health and mental illness Mental health can be defined as the actualization and maintenance of the original human nature intended by God through the

---

[119] Sun Myung Moon. "True Father to Medical Practitioners," (New York, February 3, 1987).

fulfillment of the three great blessings. Therefore, this original nature can become the standard and goal for achieving and maintaining mental health. Unification Thought defines mental illness as the condition of the human mind that has not realized the individual four position foundation. The fundamental cause of mental illness is the human fall. The consequences of this were:

1. human four position foundations are centered on Satan

2. human beings manifest fallen nature and sin

3. the relationship of the spirit and physical minds has become inverted.

4. dysfunctional human relationships have manifested

5. human beings experience psychological trauma

6. spirit persons negatively influence earthly people

All these consequences resulted in mental instability and disorders.

(5) The influence of family and environment on mental health

If the three great blessings had been fulfilled the family and the natural environment would have been conducive to mental health. Mental illness is induced within fallen families and a fallen environment.

(6) The approach for mental health maintenance

Mental health can be achieved and maintained by daily study of God's word, training sessions which include self-reflection, pure artistic activity, hobby activity with friends and family, proper nutrition, regular exercise, and holistic medical treatment.

(7) The treatment approach for mental illness

The treatment approach is to guide people to eliminate sin and fallen nature, develop latent original nature, and restore one's lineage.

(8) The goal of therapy/counseling

The goal of counseling or therapy is to eliminate sin and fallen nature, develop latent original nature, and restore one's lineage in order to achieve ultimate true mental health.

(9) Qualifications or attributes of the therapist/counselor

A counselor or therapist must have an absolutely unselfish, clear, and pure mind.

CHAPTER III   APPRAISAL OF THE THREE MODELS FROM THE UNIFICATION
THOUGHT PERSPECTIVE

Despite the emergence of various models for the maintenance of mental health and the treatment of mental illness, no ultimate cure has yet been found for problems of the mind. As stated in the introduction of this study, the Unification Thought model is capable of resolving the limitations of and integrating and harmonizing the physical, spiritual, and energetic perspectives of the models herein presented and surveyed by providing a comprehensive and holistic framework for understanding mental health and illness. This could conceivably lead to improved maintenance of mental health, more efficacious treatment of mental illness and, ultimately, the healing of mental disorders. Through the process of critically comparing the Western, Eastern, and human energy field models with the Unification Thought model, we will identify their strengths and limitations and then explain how the UT model can resolve their limitations as well as integrate and harmonize their differing perspectives.

1. Critical comparison of the explanations of the ideal human being

No attempt has been made to define an ideal human being in modern psychology. The focus has been on studying human behavior from a materialistic perspective. In fact, in Western philosophy, both ancient and modern, there is no consensus for explaining the essence of a human being.

Eastern philosophy has a clear understanding that an ideal human being is an enlightened being with an ethical, wise, and compassionate character. Such a person is naturally good and has a lifestyle in alignment with the Tao or way of Heaven. Energy healers are in agreement that an ideal human being is a manifestation of God, a being of truth and love with a mind of harmonized rational and intuitive aspects.

UT recognizes that the Western model is not able to grasp the essence of an ideal human being because the spiritual aspect of the human being is ignored or denied. The Eastern model has an accurate understanding of an ideal human being but is not aware of the relationship of heart that God wants to have with His children. Energy healers can perceive the spiritual nature of human beings and thus have a good understanding of the potential human beings have for divinity. The UT model can resolve the limited understanding of the Western and Eastern models and harmonizes with the HEF understanding.

2. Critical comparison of the models regarding the relationship between the mind and body

The assumption that human consciousness arises from the functions of the physical brain remains prevalent in the Western perspective due to the influence of materialistic theories.[120] The Western understanding has also been influenced by the long-held Christian world view that regards "spirit" as having no substance. This metaphysical assumption, which originated with Plato's view of matter and form was adopted by both St. Augustine and St. Aquinas in their theological writings which are the foundation of Christian thought. It has made it seemingly impossible to research human consciousness or spirituality with the scientific method, which observes only physical phenomena.[121] Thus, from both the scientific and religious perspective, the Western model of mental health and illness is problematic and has some limitation.

The Eastern model views spirit and matter as forming an inseparable oneness guided by cosmic consciousness. Eastern religions understand the dynamic web of the energy frequencies of the universe and clearly assert that our physical selves are a manifestation of both cosmic and human consciousness.[122] This is a correct understanding from the UT perspective.

The HEF model sees the human mind as existing within the context of the 7 human energy fields which act as a template and energetic framework for the physical body. The UT model concurs with this cause and effect understanding of the relationship between the mind and body.

Unification Thought asserts that mind and body, or spirit and matter share common elements that interact in a cause and effect as well as internal and external relationship. The mind is conscious and energetic in nature and the physical body, which is the material aspect, also has some level of consciousness even down to the cellular level.[123] Thus, the UT model solves and

---

[120] English and English, *A Comprehensive Dictionary of Psychological and Psychoanalytical Terms: A Guide to Usage,* 1st ed., 424.

[121] David Burton, Phd., "What is the Spirit?: Some Physics of Spiritual Existence." *The Unity of Sciences and Unification Thought* Vol. 8 (2006): 293.

[122] Sir John Woodroffe, *The Serpent Power* (New York: Dover, 1974), 33, quoted in Michael Talbot, *The Holographic Universe* (New York: Harper Collins, 1991), 288; and Douglas Sharon, *Wizard of the Four Winds: A Shaman's Story,* (New York: Free Press, 1978), 59, quoted in Talbot, *The Holographic Universe,* 289.

[123] UTI, *New Essentials of Unification Thought,* 105.

corrects the problematic materialistic monism theory as well as the traditional Christian world view which regards the human spirit as having no substance.

The understanding of the cosmos and of human life as a continuum of energy imbued with consciousness is emerging as a paradigm within some recent scientific theories; most notably, the theory of the holographic universe developed by physicist, David Bohm. [124] Thus, it is tenable for a conceptual bridge to be constructed between the material and spiritual realms which has heretofore not existed in western world views due to faulty metaphysical assumptions, both religious and scientific (the Christian world view and the scientific naturalism world view).

3. Critical comparison of the structure of the mind and human nature

The Western model is limited in its understanding of mental health and illness because the pioneers of the field of psychology accepted the tenets of scientific naturalism, a fundamentally materialistic world view which attempts to understand human behavior without reference to anything non-material, such as God and the human spirit, and sees all life as mechanistic and deterministic. [125] Also, a unified Western model does not exist since many disparate theories have been proposed over the 120 history of modern psychology.

The Eastern understanding of the mind recognizes dual aspects of yang and yin or rational and intuitive modes of consciousness that are in dynamic balance. This is a correct but incomplete understanding, from the UT perspective.

The 7 human energy fields described by energy healers is an energetic explanation that is in agreement with the UT perspective: there are attributes of intellect, emotion and will on both the physical and spiritual planes of human existence.

In the Western model, theorists in the field of psychology have moved away from the scientific naturalism paradigm which held sway over the last 120 years by developing more humanistic, cognitive, and spiritual theories about human behavior. However, an effective view of human nature has yet to be clarified and none have found consensus in the field of psychology. The Eastern model's understanding of human nature aligns with God's purpose of creation for

---

[124] refer to Michael Talbot's book, *The Holographic Universe*

[125] Richards and Bergin, *Spiritual Strategy*, 34.

humans and all created beings:

1. Buddhism stresses the need to strive to fulfill what UT refers to as the 1st blessing (individual perfection of heart) through mindfulness and meditation practice. In this way, the ordinary human nature, which is deluded by ignorance and the cravings of the ego, can be transformed into a Buddha (enlightened) nature.

2. Confucianism focuses on education in the 5 moral principles and the three bonds which align with the 2nd blessing (the establishment of a family in which God's love is expressed and circulates well). Propriety in family relationships are then extended to other social relationships. The human being's inherently good nature is seen to have a tendency for impropriety.

3. Taoism teaches the way to harmonize with the created world, a teaching which aligns with the 3rd blessing (dominion over the created world).

4. Shamanism understands the negative influence of spirit persons in the spirit world on earthly people and provides a way to lessen that influence which can disturb peoples' minds. UT agrees with the HEF model's understanding that human beings are unique, individual manifestations of God who desire and seek a connection with the divine. But humans also have free will, and can choose to either follow divine guidance or shut off the higher flow of energy and thus become ego-centered.

The UT model of the harmonized spirit mind and physical mind is more clear and complete than the Western and Eastern models and it agrees with the energetic perspective. However, further research is needed in order to more fully elucidate the structure of the human mind.

The UT model provides a clear, God-centered understanding of original human nature that solves the problematic, unclarified Western view. UT's three great blessings are mirrored in Eastern religious practice. And, the UT concept of the original mind resonates with the HEF understanding of the higher self. Thus, the three models can be integrated and harmonized by the UT perspective.

4. Critical comparison of definitions of mental health and mental illness

The Western model has standard definitions for mental health but is not clear on how to achieve them.

      1. absence of mental illness

      2. appropriate social behavior

      3. freedom from worry and guilt

      4. personal competence and control

      5. self-acceptance and self-actualization

      6. unification and organization of personality

      7. open-mindedness and flexibility[126]

The UT model clarifies how to achieve these definitions of mental health because it is more holistic and comprehensive. The UT perspective has constructs that explain how to achieve the Western definitions as follows:

1) "Absence of mental disorder" can be achieved when the spirit mind and the physical mind of an individual harmoniously center on God's heart (thus forming the original mind) (1st blessing) and when such individuals form harmonious families (2nd blessing) which are a wholesome environment for spiritual growth. Giving love and care to all things also promotes mental health (3rd blessing).

2) "Appropriate social behavior" is that behavior which can be experienced and learned in families where God's love and norms are expressed (2nd blessing). From the UT perspective, family members can grow and mature through experiencing the realms of children's love, sibling love, conjugal love between husband and wife, and parental love.

3) "Absence of guilt, worry, or anxiety" can be realized by taking personal responsibility to restore one's original human nature. In other words, an individual should recognize and acknowledge (confess and repent in religious terms) unprincipled thoughts, feelings, and behaviors and then strive to break bad habits and establish good habits of thought, feeling, and behavior.

---

[126] R.F. Paloutzian, *Invitation to the Psychology of Religion*, (London: Allyn and Bacon, 1996), 253.

4) "Self-control and competence" are realized by harmonizing one's spirit and physical mind through mind and body unity practice and disciplining one's self to overcome self-centered desires. (1st blessing)

5) "Self-acceptance and self-actualization" can be realized by striving to resemble God's parental heart and sacrificial character through thinking of others before one's self. (1st blessing)

6) An "organized and unified personality" can be realized when one's physical mind and physical life conforms to the impulse of one's spirit mind in harmonious give and receive action. (intellect, emotion, and will are balanced and centered on a heart of true love) (1st blessing)

7) An "open and flexible" mind can be realized through the expression of original human nature; that is, by expressing God's compassionate, parental heart, keeping "connected being consciousness," and multiplying goodness.

The Eastern model sees individual enlightenment, propriety in relationships, alignment with the way of nature, and harmony with the spirit world as four ways of being mentally healthy. The UT model explains how the Buddhist, Confucianist, and Taoist understanding of mental health, when combined, align with God's three great blessings to humankind. However, there is some limitation from the UT perspective. The precious and sacred value of the Eastern faith traditions can be greatly augmented by harmonizing with Unification Thought which more fully elucidates God's nature, the original human nature and how it became mis-directed, and humankind's relationship with the Spirit World.

UT affirms and accepts as valid the HEF model's energetic definition of mental health which focuses on clearing, balancing, and synchronizing the human energy fields.

Presently, the biological model is generally used to explain mental health and illness in the Western model. It is thought that mental disorders arise from an imbalance of brain chemicals. [127] However, this theory is unproven and intuitively inadequate. From the UT perspective it is a partial and limited understanding due to its focus on physical symptoms rather than on the underlying causes. The UT model more clearly defines mental illness and identifies

---

[127] Robert Whitaker. interview by Terry Messman, *Street Spirit*, (Oakland, California, 2010), 3.

causes which the Western model completely fails to recognize due to its generally materialistic understanding and its exclusive focus on symptoms. Thus, UT can resolve its limitations.

In the Eastern model, Buddhism understands the cause of mental illness as ignorance, cravings, and the deceptions of the ego. In fact, Buddhists see our collective human ignorance manifesting as collective mental illness, a perspective which the UT model would accept as valid. That is because our so called "human condition" is not "natural" and therefore, certainly not healthy. It is a fallen nature, not the original nature as intended by God. The yearning of our latent original mind causes many to ponder about and strive for a lost ideal that ought to be.

Confucianism teaches that impropriety is the root of disorder in human relationships. Taoism recognizes a lack of alignment with the Way, and Shamanism regards the influence of troublesome spirits as the source of mental disturbance. Each of these faith traditions have revealed deep insights into the causes of mental illness which resonate with the causes described in the UT model. In essence, each faith tradition sees one aspect of the unfilled ideal of the three great blessings which have led to unhappiness and mental suffering. However, from the Unification perspective there are limitations in all these understandings. Buddhism, Confucianism, Taoism and Shamanism are ancient belief systems which:

1. do not have a clear conception of God who is the Parent of all humankind,

2. do not have a clear understanding of the human fall which is the root cause of human ignorance, delusion, impropriety, and spiritual disturbance,

3. do not have a clear understanding of the spiritual world and its interaction with earthly people.

These limitations of understanding can be resolved by accepting and harmonizing with the more comprehensive UT understanding.

The HEF model recognizes the distortion or imbalance among the human energy fields as caused by:

1. selfish intentions

2. avoidance of pain

3. erroneous beliefs

which block our divine essence from flowing through our being. This is a correct understanding from the UT perspective but the UT understanding is more comprehensive in that it explains why, through the motivation and process of the human fall, our intentions became mostly self-centered so that all people's energy fields need healing.

5. Critical comparison of the models regarding the influence of family and environment on mental health

The Western model does not have a clear understanding of influences on mental health because it is limited to a social scientific perspective that tends to ignore the spiritual nature of human beings. The Eastern model's understanding is closer to the three great blessings. It is understood in Eastern faith traditions that human beings are not living according to the Way of Heaven and need to correct their path in life as individuals and in relationship to others and the natural world. Energy healers recognize that we have habits of negatively interacting with and manipulating others which they can see in people's energy fields. They see that we have also become more and more disconnected from the energies of the natural world. They guide people to heal the damage done to their energy fields. Since the UT model has a clear understanding of ideal relationships as well as "fallen" relationships and how to restore them, UT can resolve the limitation of the Western model and integrate the Eastern and HEF models into its more comprehensive view.

6. Critical comparison of the approaches for mental health maintenance

Psychologists and psychiatrists generally recognize the need for proper nutrition and regular exercise which are two of the eight elements the UT model recommends for maintaining mental health. However, in the Western model there is an ever-increasing dependence on pharmaceutical drugs for mental health maintenance. This dependence is very problematic due to their questionable efficacy and harmful side effects. This is a serious limitation from the UT perspective. The UT model affirms the Western recommendation of regular exercise and proper nutrition as part of mental health maintenance but does not support the on-going trend of the over-dependence on pharmaceutical drugs.

From the perspective of the Eastern model, mental health can be maintained through mindful meditation in Buddhism, practicing the 5 principles and 3 bonds of Confucianism, and aligning with the way of nature as taught by Taoism. Eastern faith traditions, when combined, have therefore been guiding people to fulfill the three great blessings, God's original ideal for humankind. However, there are some limitations from the Unification perspective mentioned previously. Nonetheless, the wisdom of these faith traditions is immense and of great value in guiding humankind toward realizing its vast potential as children who resemble and resonate with their Parent, God.

The UT understanding acknowledges the need for people to seek harmony with their ancestors and the spirit world. However, Shamans are not able to permanently bring harmony or resolve negative influence from the spirit world due to lack of a full understanding of the spirit world. The more comprehensive UT understanding can resolve the limitation of Shamanism.

The HEF model emphasizes consciously balancing our energy fields. Two aspects of this approach are doing occasional self-inventories (self-reflection) to identify imbalances and keeping oneself grounded and present in the here and now. The UT model recognizes these as helpful practices but they are not sufficiently comprehensive. This limitation would be resolved by integrating with the eight necessary elements of the UT approach.

7. Critical comparison of the treatment approaches for mental illness

The current treatment of choice in the Western model is the prescribing of pharmaceutical drugs for the purpose of balancing brain chemicals. The standard protocol is simply to maintain mental balance with man-made, chemical drugs. Psychiatrists will readily admit that they believe that mental disorders are incurable and that mental patients should, therefore, remain on medication throughout their physical lives![128] Surely, chemical imbalances in the brain are merely an effect or symptom of some deeper, underlying cause. Furthermore, this cause has yet to be determined by western science. There are no standard medical tests for determining the presence of mental illness despite the preferred biological model. Diagnosis is dependent on an interview and the observation of a patient's attitude and behavior by a psychiatrist who has a manual of symptoms linked to names of disorders.[129] The efficacy of this approach is at best questionable. And, there is much evidence that the use of psychiatric drugs leads to various adverse outcomes such as weight gain, psychotic breaks, permanent brain

---

[128] Robert Whitaker. interview, 4.
[129] Robert L. Spitzer, MD., *Diagnostic and Statistical Manual of Mental Disorders*, 3rded. (Washington, D.C., American Psychiatric Association,1980).

damage, and suicidal ideation, etc.[130] It is certainly a limited understanding and often a harmful approach. The UT model can clarify the underlying causes of mental disorders and thus resolve this limitation. It also has the capability to evaluate and systematize the various psycho-therapeutic approaches based on an understanding of the original human nature, the human fall, and the restoration of the three great blessings.[131]

In the Eastern model, meditation is used as a tool for exploring consciousness and also a means of transforming it, in order to purge the mind of mental toxins such as cravings, anger, envy, etc. The UT model sees this as a very helpful approach. However, the Shamanist approach with its ceremonies and rituals (to appease the spirits) can only provide a temporary solution; it cannot permanently resolve a mental disorder. The UT understanding and approach for solving negative influence from the spirit world can provide a permanent solution.

HEF healers can repair the distorted human energy fields and guide patients to repair their own fields using thought processes such as meditation, affirmation, and visualization. They believe that selfish intention or avoidance of psychological pain blocks the flow of divine essence in the energy fields which can lead to mental and physical illness. But they do not take into consideration the harmful influence of vengeful spirits upon earthly people. The UT model acknowledges the value of the energetic approach, but this lack of recognition of the influence of spirits is a serious limitation. Once the HEF model integrates with the UT understanding and approach, this limitation can be resolved. Thus, the UT model has the capability to harmonize the Western, Eastern, and energetic treatment approaches for mental disorders.

8. Critical comparison of the goals for therapy/counseling

The Western over-dependence on synthetic medications for maintaining the balance of brain chemicals cannot be considered an adequate goal for healing from the UT perspective. Furthermore, because the Western model does not have a unified psycho-therapeutic or counseling approach, it means that the goal of therapy or counseling is also not unified, but instead dependent on the value system of each individual therapist. This is also seen as a serious

---

[130] For a full investigation of the history of psychiatric care in America, refer to Robert Whitaker's book, *Mad in America: Bad Science, Bad Medicine, and the Enduring Mistreatment of the Mentally Ill.*

[131] For pioneering work in this regard, refer to Dr. Yuji Ootomo's *Completed Testament Pastoral Counseling* lecture series and Robert and Janice Maddox' book, *Deep Origin Healing and the Origin of Personality Distortion.*

weakness from the UT perspective which advocates a unified value system centered upon God's true love.

The goal of healing from the Eastern perspective is enlightenment for Buddhists, propriety in relationships in Confucianism, and harmony with nature or the spiritual realm for Taoists and those who seek the aid of Shamans. Taken together, these are similar to the goals of the UT model which is based upon the ideal of the three great blessings. However, the UT approach is more comprehensive and can lead to an ultimate solution for mental disorders through the restoration of the three great blessings, the Spirit World, and God's lineage.

The HEF model's goal for healing is to keep the human energy fields clear, balanced, and synchronized so as to enable the divine essence to be able to flow smoothly for the optimum functioning of the mind and body. The UT model recognizes the validity of this goal because of its emphasis on balanced relationships on all levels of human existence, starting with the relationship of the spirit and physical minds centering upon God's heart of true love.

The UT model proposes and advocates an absolute standard and goal for mental health as well as a lasting cure for mental illness. The goal for achieving and maintaining mental health is to grow towards the actualization of one's original human nature which is latent and undeveloped in our spirit mind. The goal for the healing of mental illness, which all human beings experience, is the eradication of the sin and fallen nature in one's self and one's ancestors which can lead to the restoration of one's lineage back to God's lineage from which our original human ancestors departed. The other models have some partial insights into this understanding but need to adopt the more comprehensive UT understanding in order to achieve "true mental health," as seen from God's perspective.

9. Critical comparison of qualifications or attributes of the therapist/counselor/healer

In the Western model, psychologists and psychiatrists are trained based on a generally materialistic (physical) perspective of mental health and illness, and therefore their understanding is limited. The UT model is significantly more comprehensive in that therapists and counselors should exemplify God's heart of true love and fully understand the root cause of mental illness (the human fall) and how to restore mental health based upon the standard of the original human nature.

In the Eastern model, counselors are exemplary guides who are adept at self-mastery and achieve states of enlightenment which they train others to strive for. Most shamans are called and tested before they begin training. Such qualifications are imperative from the UT perspective.

In the HEF model, energy healers have broad training not only in energetic healing techniques but in psychology, human physiology, ethics, and a holistic world view. UT acknowledges that their qualifications are very good.

The UT model can provide the lacking aspects of the Western, Eastern, and energy therapist's training with its more holistic and God-centered understanding. By correcting erroneous metaphysical assumptions and completing the partial understandings of these models, the UT perspective can harmonize and unify them for the sake of all humankind and ultimately for God's sake.

3 models critically compared from the UT perspective

categories \ models	Western	Eastern	HEF	UT
1. the ideal human being	X	p	O	O
2. relationship between mind and body	X	O	O	O
3. structure of the mind and human nature	X	p	O	O
4. definitions of MH & MI	p	O	O	O
5. influence of family and environment on mental health	p	p	p	O
6. mental health maintenance approach	p	p	p	O
7. treatment approach for mental illness	X	p	p	O
8. goal of therapy/counseling/ healing	X	p	O	O
9. qualification of therapist/ counselor/healer	X	O	O	O
Perspective of model:	Focus on physical body	Focus on human spirit	Focus on human energy fields	physical, spirit, human energy fields, integrated & harmonized

key: X = insufficient   p = partial   O = sufficient

CHAPTER IV   A PROPOSAL FOR A UNIFICATION THOUGHT PARADIGM FOR "TRUE MENTAL HEALTH"

In order to completely solve any problem related to humankind, we must understand it and work to resolve it from God's point of view, carrying out God's solution through the fulfillment of our own individual portion of responsibility. This is because we are God's children whom He created to be His willing love partners for the purpose of realizing eternal joy and happiness.

Therefore, in order to solve "problems of the mind," we need to overcome our ignorance about God's original ideal of the three great blessings and how it was lost through the human fall. We need to recognize the consequences of the human fall which brought about the blockage of the circulation of God's love in the human mind and in all relationships involving human beings. And then, we need to implement God's solution for rectifying this tragic and regretful situation which has been passed down from generation to generation through the blood lineage since the original human ancestors deviated from God's ideal.

The Unification Thought model of mental health and illness is not just a theoretical model based on one individual's ideas. It is actually God's viewpoint about mental health and illness, revealed through Father Moon. Thus, with the Unification Thought model of mental health and illness as a standard, all other models can and should be appraised.

Simply stated, the ultimate cure for mental illness or "problems of the mind" is to restore Godly, true love-centered relationships which are harmonious and mutually beneficial. It is necessary for all human beings to learn, believe, and practice God's way of life and love in order to maintain mental health, and to solve "problems of the mind" if humankind is to see this hereditary and historical problem eradicated.

God's heart yearns, and seeks unceasingly, for the resolution of "problems of the mind" and the restoration of the original human nature latent within human beings. As Robert and Janice Maddox point out,

> God is deeply longing for people to take responsibility, because, ultimately, to bridge the gap from God to humanity, each of us has to learn to embody true love. This is not a job of just one person who does

it all for us. ...[W]e each have to become the bridge for our lineage."[132]

Until such resolution and restoration takes place, God and humankind will continuously experience mental torment, suffering, and misery.

It need not be a matter of faith alone to accept the UT theology of the fall and its philosophy of mental health and illness because this perspective proves tenable when subjected to the hypothetical method.[133]

Here, we summarize the basic tenets of the UT model which shed new light for understanding mental health and illness:

1. Explanation of an ideal human being:

An ideal human being is a person with a mature, loving character who is living according to the Way of Heaven and desiring to live with and return joy to God by resembling His nature. An ideal human being matures a loving character aligned with the Way of Heaven and resembles God's nature of true love through the realization of the three great blessings given by God. Through the human portion of responsibility, an individual forms an individual four position foundation of harmonized spirit mind and physical mind thus forming the original mind. Children are guided in their growth toward fulfilling the first blessing in God-centered families in which the parents have achieved the ideal of true parents through the unity of husband and wife centered upon God's heart (the 2nd blessing). Such families give loving care to the created world as well (the 3rd blessing). Living according to God's fundamental principle of give and receive action for the sake of realizing goodness, family relationships are meant to be the foundation of a heavenly world both on Earth and in the spiritual world. UT calls this "one cosmic family under God" ("Cheon Il Guk" in Korean).

2. The ideal mind and body relationship:

The human mind and body have elements in common so they are able to interact. UT explains the relationship of dual characteristics within God and all created beings; there is an

---

[132] Robert and Janice Maddox, *Deep Origin Healing*, 181.
[133] Jennifer Tanabe, *Contemplating Unification Thought*, (Barrytown, N.Y.: Unification Theological Seminary, 1993), 1.

inner nature which directs the external form. This understanding resolves the incorrect Western view which holds that spirit has nothing in common with matter, but that spirit or consciousness is generated from matter (materialistic monism).

3. The structure of the mind and human nature

The spirit mind and the physical mind are designed to relate harmoniously centered upon God's motivation of heart thus establishing a four position foundation of goodness where intellect, emotion and will function in a balanced way. Growing towards and achieving resonance or oneness with God's heart is fundamental for true mental health. Human nature is meant to express truth, beauty, goodness and unselfish love. It is the nature that returns joy to God according to the desires of the original mind.

4. The definition of mental health and mental illness

The original "ideal" human nature, as intended by God, is the standard and goal for achieving and maintaining true mental health. It is the nature to maintain God's heart and viewpoint, live according to connected-being consciousness, and multiply only goodness. Until now, the Western view has been to strive only for relative mental health based on a relativistic understanding of human nature. Buddhist teaching understands that we should seek for ultimate mental health, that is, enlightenment (which means becoming aware of the nature of our true, original self and striving to actualize it). UT concurs with the Buddhist view.

Unification Thought defines mental illness as the condition of the human mind that has not realized the individual four position foundation. In other words, the desires of the spirit mind and physical mind are not harmonized centered upon God's love and the Way of Heaven but are instead in conflict and separated from God. This is because, due to the fall, the originally intended subject and object relationship of the spirit mind and the physical mind became reversed. The physical mind's self-oriented desires, rather than being pursued in a harmonious relationship with the spirit mind, dominate the spirit mind's desires for truth, beauty and goodness. The flow of true, unselfish, and properly ordered love became blocked and/or distorted so that human beings suffer and experience internal contradiction as well as conflicts in relationships. Therefore, the human fall and its consequences are clearly the root cause of mental illness.

As spiritual beings, earthly people are not only influenced by other earthly people but also by passed-away spirit persons. Until today, all people have passed into the spirit world with the same fallen nature and sin with which they were burdened on earth, and they continue to express it in the spirit world. Most spirit persons desire to take revenge upon the descendants of those who harmed them by causing both physical and mental suffering. This is another major cause of mental illness which has not been resolved because, until now, there has been no way to restore troublesome spirits.

5. The influence of family and environment on mental health

The family is meant to be the school of true love that teaches norms based on the Way of Heaven for relating to others in the greater society as well as with the natural world. It is within the family that God's ideal of the three great blessings is to be realized and mental health maintained. But because Satan came to dominate the four position foundations of the individual, family, and all things (through fallen people), mis-directed, false love as well as false beliefs and norms have multiplied from generation to generation which has inevitably led to the collective mental illness of humankind in the form of fallen nature and sin.

6. The approach for mental health maintenance

Father Moon's recommendations for achieving and maintaining mental health are comprehensive and holistic including proper nutrition and regular exercise, wholesome hobby and artistic activity, holistic medical treatment, and self-reflection and training in mind and body unity. Most notably, his number one recommendation is to study God's words recorded in religious scriptures. By doing so as a daily habit, human beings can direct their lives with a clear understanding of the purpose and meaning of their existence as well as a clear standard of ethics and morality for attaining that purpose based on the laws of the universe, also known as the Way of Heaven.

7. The treatment approach for mental illness

Dr. Yuji Ootomo, the pioneer of a UT counseling approach, proposes that the goal of counseling be the decrease and ultimate elimination of fallen nature while developing and strengthening original nature that has been latent within human beings since the creation of humankind. To accomplish this it is necessary and important to be aware of and reflect about one's thoughts and feelings; to learn to discern original and fallen nature in one's self and in others in order to "separate the trash." It is very important to not respond with fallen nature when others express fallen nature. Instead, we should stimulate the other person's original nature by expressing original nature towards them. Dr. Ootomo emphasizes that we who are living today have the responsibility to restore our lineage in order to break the historical, hereditary cycle of anxiety and anger--- which he sees as the common denominator of problems of the mind---so that it is not passed on to our descendants. Father Moon has said that, "All people of the world have the responsibility to take down the walls of grudges and resentments their ancestors built up...."[134]

Robert and Janice Maddox, through their study, research, and healing experience have combined Divine Principle insights about our human ancestor's separation from God with psycho-dynamic and human energy field perspectives. They see fallen natures as the root energies for personality distortions, also known as defenses. The emotional healing process they have developed involves three fundamental steps of self-awareness through objective introspection and self-examination, the disintegration of defenses, and the reintegration of one's original mind or higher self, thus establishing healthy thought patterns, habits and behaviors. Both Dr. Ootomo and the Maddox couple recognize that individuals involved in their healing approaches must be willing to take on the responsibility for ending the vicious cycle of fallen nature in their lineage.

Due to the merit of the age in God's providence to restore humankind, a way has now been opened to resolve a major cause of mental illness, that is, mental disturbance caused by fallen spirit persons. This is the spiritual works of liberating and restoring spirit persons attached to earthly persons centering upon the Cheongpyeong Heaven and Earth Training Center

---

[129] Thomas G. Walsh, publisher. *World Scripture and the Teachings of Sun Myung Moon.* (New York: Universal Peace Federation, 2011), 276.

established by our True Parents, Father and Mother Moon, in South Korea.

In order to ultimately eradicate mental illness from humankind, all people in the physical world and spirit world need to restore their blood lineage back to God. An essential part of that restoration process is to participate as engaged or married couples in the Marriage Blessing Ceremony, the ceremony for receiving the forgiveness of original sin established by Father and Mother Moon, the True Parents of Heaven, Earth and humankind, acknowledged by God.

8. The goal of therapy/counseling/healing

When dealing with problems of the mind or dysfunctional relationships the issues cannot be fully resolved without addressing the underlying cause and striving for the ultimate goal of becoming an ideal human being according to the desires of our original mind. There are four aspects for achieving this goal:

    1) Eliminate fallen nature and 3 kinds of sin

    2) Develop latent original nature

    3) Restore one's lineage beginning with the parent/child
       relationship

    4) Ultimately, receive the forgiveness of original sin from the
       True Parents in order to return to God's blood lineage

9. Qualifications or attributes of the therapist/counselor

Fundamentally, a counselor needs to have a pure heart and accepts and practices the UT approach.

The UT approach opens a way for human beings, as God's children, to ultimately realize true mental health. They can be guided by mentors who are themselves devoted to fulfilling the three great blessings and restoring themselves and their lineage.

Only by believing and practicing God's truth, and then resolving false forms of love as well as anger and anxiety (which is provoked by experiences of false love) can the historical, hereditary and collective problem of mental illness be solved. Only then will God and His children, as well as all created beings, be liberated from a false lineage, a false dominion, and a false environment from which problems of the mind arise and a true lineage, true dominion, and a true environment be established. Thus, a God-centered and true love-centered paradigm is imperative and essential for mental illness to be cured once and for all.

CHAPTER V   CONCLUSION AND DIRECTIONS FOR FUTURE RESEARCH

The comprehensive and holistic UT model of mental health and illness is sufficient for creating a new paradigm and providing an approach for ultimately solving mental illness and guiding people to achieve true mental health.

We have argued that an appraisal of the various approaches for promoting mental health and treating mental illness is needed due to the lack of a cure for mental illness which has been plaguing humanity throughout human history. Erroneous metaphysical assumptions and incomplete world views have prevented a unified and truly efficacious approach from being realized.

We have argued that Unification Thought can provide a systematic framework for appraising the Western, Eastern, and alternative human energy field models for mental health and illness. We have utilized nine categories for surveying and then critically comparing these models with the Unification Thought model.

In Chapter I, the Western, Eastern, and human energy field models were presented. These models can be categorized as physical, spiritual, and energetic perspectives, respectively. After surveying these models, we concluded that none of them are sufficiently comprehensive or holistic in their understanding and approach and thus cannot ultimately provide a cure for mental illness.

In Chapter II, we presented a Unification Thought model which is comprehensive and holistic in its understanding and approach.

In Chapter III, we appraised the Western, Eastern, and human energy field models. We pointed out their limitations and strengths from the UT perspective and we explained how the UT model can resolve their limitations and integrate and harmonize their strengths.

In Chapter IV, we summarized the basic tenets of the UT model's paradigm for "true mental health." Once this new paradigm is accepted, studied, and put into practice, it will become possible to restore the ideal of the three great blessings in the physical world, as well as to restore the spirit world and God's lineage of true love.

Thus, we can conclude that the UT model does indeed stand as the "true mental health" paradigm which needs to be tested and proven through further research. The Cheongpyeong training center would be an appropriate starting place for researching the efficacy of this proposed paradigm's treatment approach. Many trainees have already testified, including this author, that healing of mental illness is taking place.

Through this study, we have highlighted essential and fundamental realizations about the human condition that need to be sincerely considered and addressed if "problems of the mind"---that have plagued all people without exception---are to be solved. This study is intended to be a formation stage or a point of departure from which to identify and pursue further avenues for research and development of this proposed paradigm.

The following are some aspects of the UT paradigm for true mental health which need further research and development:

1) Further research and systematization of Father Moon's teaching about mental health and illness

2) Case studies examining the efficacy of Dr. Ootomo's counseling approach for improving mental health and resolving dysfunctional relationships

3) Development, application, and assessment of the "DEEP Origin emotional process" healing approach based upon the fallen nature/defenses theory proposed by Robert and Janice Maddox

4) Case studies assessing the efficacy of the treatment for mental illness at Cheongpyeong Heaven and Earth Training Center in   collaboration with Cheongshim International Medical Center in South Korea

5) A systematic elucidation of the human spirit mind and spirit body

6) A systematic elucidation of the relationship between the human spirit self and the physical self

7) A systematic elucidation of the spirit world's influence on earthly people

8) Elucidation of the restoration process for spirit persons in the spirit world

9) Elucidation of the phenomenon of "returning spirit resurrection"

10) Appraisal and systematization of psychotherapeutic theories from the UT perspective

11) Creation of workshop presentations, workbooks, and other educational materials for therapists and those who seek healing

12) Creation of websites, webinars, blogs, and other online resources

We encourage all those interested in developing UT Psychology to collaborate in the research and development of these aspects of the "true mental health" paradigm and approach.

BIBLIOGRAPHY

Brennan, Barbara. *Light Emerging: The Journey of Personal Healing.* New York: Bantam Books, 1993.

Burton, David. "What is Spirit?: Some Physics of Spiritual Existence." *Proceedings of the International Symposium on Unification Thought: The Unity of Sciences and Unification Thought,* vol. 8. Edited by Unification Thought Institute. Korea: UTI-Korea, 2006.

Capra, Fritjof. *The Tao of Physics: An Exploration of the Parallels Between Modern Physics and Eastern Mysticism.* New York: Bantam Books, 1975.

Cheongpyeong Heaven and Earth Training Center. *In Search of the True Self* 3rd ed. Seorak-myeon: Cheongpyeong Training Center, 2007.

Dubs, G. "Psycho-spiritual development in Zen Buddhism: A study of resistance in meditation." *Journal of Transpersonal Psychology,* 19 (1987), 19-87, quoted in Groth-Marnat, Gary. "Buddhism and Mental Health: A Comparative Analysis." In *Religion and Mental Health,* edited by John F. Schumaker, 272. New York: Oxford University Press, 1992.

Epstein, Mark. *Thoughts without a Thinker: Psychotherapy from a Buddhist Perspective.* New York: Basic Books, 1995.

Family Federation for World Peace and Unification. *Cheon Seong Gyeong: Selections from the Speeches of True Parents.* Seoul: FFWPU, 2006.

Groth-Marnat, Gary. "Buddhism and Mental Health: A Comparative Analysis." In *Religion and Mental Health,* edited by John F. Schumaker, 272. New York: Oxford University Press, 1992.

Ishii, Hiroshi. *The Mind-Brain Problem and Unification Thought.* Seoul:Unification Thought Institute, 2008.

Krasner, L. "The Therapist as a Social Reinforcement Machine." *Research in Psychotherapy* (vol. 2), edited by H.H. Strupp & L. Luborsky, 61-94. Washington, D.C.: American Psychological Association, 1962. Quoted in P. Scott Richards and Allen E. Bergin, *A Spiritual Strategy for Counseling and Psychotherapy.* 2nd ed. Washington, D.C.: American Psychological Association, 2005.

Maddox, Robert and Janice. *D.E.E.P. ORIGIN HEALING and the Origin of Personality Distortion.* U.S.A.: D' Har Services, 2012.

Martin, Barbara, and Dimitri Moraitis. *Change Your Aura Change Your Life: A Step-by-Step Guide to Unfolding Your Spiritual Power.* Sunland, CA: WisdomLight Books, 2003.

McLaren, Karla. *Your Aura & Your Chakras: the Owner' s Manual.* Boston: Weiser Books, 1998.

Modi, Shakuntala. *Remarkable Healings; A Psychiatrist Discovers Unsuspected Roots of Mental and Physical Illness.* Charlottesville, VA: Hampton Roads Publishing Company, Inc., 1997.

Moon, Sun Myung. *True Families, Gateway to Heaven*. New York: H.S.A.-U.W.C., 2009.

Olsen, Gwen. "The Mission-Gwen Olsen-the Rx Reformer,
    http://www.youtube.com/watch?v=j4byng7x7Kk, (accessed July 15, 2011.)

Otani, Akifumi. "Beyond Freudianism." *Paper presented at the 23rd International Symposium on Unification Thought: The Unity of Sciences and Unification Thought: Towards Exploring Unification Thought Academic Disciplines,* Japan: UTI-Japan, 2011.

Ootomo, Yuji. "Completed Testament Pastoral Counseling: The Psychology of Tribal Witnessing" lecture series, 2011.

Paloutzian, R.F. *Invitation to the Psychology of Religion*. 2nd ed. London: Allyn and Bacon, 1996.

Richards, P. Scott and Allen E. Bergin, *A Spiritual Strategy for Counseling and Psychotherapy*, 2nd ed. Washington, D.C.: American Psychological Association, 2005.

Seligman, M.E.P. "Positive Psychology, Positive Prevention, and Positive Therapy," *Handbook of Positive Psychology*, edited by C.R. Snyder & S.J. Lopez, 3-9. New York: Oxford University Press, 2002.

Sharon, Douglas. *Wizard of the Four Winds: A Shaman's Story*. New York: Free Press, 1978.

Sperry, R.W. "Psychology's Mentalist Paradigm and the Religion/Science Tension." *American Psychologist*, 43 (1988): 607-613, quoted in P. Scott Richards and Allen E. Bergin, *A Spiritual Strategy for Counseling and Psychotherapy*. 2nd ed. Washington, D.C.: American Psychological Association, 2005.

Spitzer, Robert L. *Diagnostic and Statistical Manual of Mental Disorders,* 3rd ed. Washington, D.C., American Psychiatric Association, 1980.

Talbot, Michael. *The Holographic Universe*. New York: HarperCollins, 1991.

The Holy Spirit Association for the Unification of World Christianity. *Exposition of the Divine Principle*. New York: H.S.A.-U.W.C., revised edition, 2006.

Unification Thought Institute (UTI). *New Essentials of Unification Thought; Head-Wing Thought*. Bridgeport, CT: The Research Institute of the Integration of World Thought, 2006.

Walsh, Thomas G., publisher. *World Scripture and the Teachings of Sun Myung Moon*. New York: Universal Peace Federation, 2011.

Watson, J.B. *Psychology from the Standpoint of a Behaviorist*. Dover, N.H.: Frances Pinter, 1983 (Original work published 1924). Quoted in P. Scott Richards and Allen E. Bergin, *A Spiritual Strategy for Counseling and Psychotherapy*. 2nd ed. Washington, D.C.: American Psychological Association, 2005.

Whitaker, Robert. *Mad in America: Bad Science, Bad Medicine, and the Enduring Mistreatment of the Mentally Ill.* New York: Basic Books, 2002.

Woodroffe, Sir John. *The Serpent Power.* New York: Dover, 1974.

Yoon, Do Young. *True Father on Mental Health (research in progress): Chapter 4, How to Achieve Mental Health.* Seorak-myeon, South Korea: Cheongshim Graduate School of Theology, 2009.

http://en.wikipedia.org/wiki/chemical_imbalance (accessed July 10, 2012)

http://en.wikipedia.org/wiki/Mental_health_professional (accessed July 10, 2012)

<ABSTRACT>

A STUDY OF MODELS OF MENTAL HEALTH AND ILLNESS WITH AN APPRAISAL FROM THE UNIFICATION THOUGHT PERSPECTIVE, TOWARDS A GOD-CENTERED PARADIGM

PAULA PETERSEN-FUJIWARA
Department of Cheon Il Guk Spirituality Studies
Cheongshim Graduate School of Theology
Advisor: Professor David A. Carlson

There is a great need today for an appraisal of the various approaches taken for the promotion of mental health and the treatment of mental illness. This is because these various approaches are not well-harmonized due to their opposing metaphysical assumptions and the partial world views associated with them. As a result, mental illness---which has afflicted people throughout human history---has yet to be cured and is, in fact, spreading more rampantly as time passes. Moreover, some treatment approaches in use today are doing more harm than good due, in large part, to their erroneous and unproven theoretical assumptions.

In this study, nine categories are utilized for comparing and appraising differing models of mental health and illness from the Unification Thought (UT) perspective which originates from the teachings of the Rev. Dr. Sun Myung Moon. The categories are as follows:

1. Explanation of the ideal human being

2. The relationship between the mind and body

3. The structure of the mind and human nature

4. Definition of mental health and mental illness

5. The influence of family and environment on mental health

6. The approach for mental health maintenance

7. The treatment approach for mental illness

8. The goal of therapy/counseling

9. Qualifications or attributes of the therapist/counselor/healer

The models of mental health and illness which are examined and appraised include the Western, Eastern, and human energy field perspectives. Through this process, it becomes apparent that it is possible for the Unification Thought model to resolve the limitations of the aforementioned models and integrate and harmonize these physical, spiritual, and energetic perspectives. The UT model provides a comprehensive and holistic framework for better understanding mental health and illness. Thus, it can conceivably lead to improved mental health maintenance, to more efficacious treatment of mental illness, and ultimately, to a cure for all mental disorders. The UT model is therefore presented as a new paradigm for "true mental health."

key words: mental health, mental illness, Unification Thought, Rev. Moon, appraisal of models, Western, Eastern, human energy fields, maintenance, treatment, cure.